THE GEMINI RISING
ROCKIN' MACHINE

BOOK SIX: DO YOU REMEMBER
ROCK AND ROLL &
BOOK SEVEN: ROCK AND ROLL
BACHELOR

**Book Six: Do You Remember Rock And Roll
& Book Seven: Rock And Roll Bachelor
Copyright 2014 by The Gemini Rising Rockin' Machine
ISBN-13: 978-0692285589 (Gemini Rising Rockin'
Machine,The)
ISBN-10: 069228558X**

For questions, comments you may send correspondence to.

thegeminirisingrockinmachine@twc.com

**Official Website
www.thegeminirisingrockinmachine.com**

Failure To Rock (856.) (New Cover Bonus)

Rock-On – Rock and Roll
Scream-It-Out-Loud
Southern-Fry-It – Cali-Bake-It
Motor-City-Burn-It
Rock and Roll will Never-Die

No – Not-You – You-Don't-Rock
Can't-Feel that Sound
Inside-Your – Mind and Heart
Too-Bad for You – 'Cause-I'm-The
Rock-Hard – That-Never-Stops – Rocking
So – Rock – Off

(Chorus)
You've Been Busted
For Failure To Rock
You Suck So Bad – Because
You've Been Busted
For Failure To Rock
Ain't No Helping You – Non-Rocker

Rock-On – Rock and Roll
Scream-It-Out-Loud
Southern-Fry-It – Cali-Bake-It
Motor-City-Burn-It
Rock and Roll will Never-Die

No – Not-You – You-Don't-Rock
Can't-Feel that Sound
Inside-Your – Mind and Heart
Too-Bad for You – 'Cause-I'm the
Rock-Hard – That-Never-Stops – Rocking
So – Rock – Off

(Chorus)
You've Been Busted
For Failure To Rock
You Suck So Bad – Because
You've Been Busted
For Failure To Rock
Ain't No Helping You – Non-Rocker

Rock My Bone (908.) (New Cover Bonus)

I-Could-Tell-You – My-Sign
I-Could-Tell-You – My-Favorite-Color
I-Could-Even – Tell-You – My-Name
But-That's-Not – My-Style – No – Not-At-All

My-Style-Baby – Is-Getting-It-On
So-What – Do-You-Say – Baby
Do-You – Do-You – Do-You-Want-To
Rock My Bone

(Chorus)
Come On Baby – Rock My Bone
It's Such A Great Bone To Rock
Come On Baby – Rock My Bone
If You Say No – Baby
I'll Let Some Other Hottie
Fall In Love With – Rockin' My Bone
So Come On Baby – Rock My Bone
Before You Lose Your Chance
At Rockin' Along With The Perfect Bone

I-Could-Tell-You – My-Sign
I-Could-Tell-You-My – Favorite-Color
I-Could-Even – Tell-You – My-Name
But-That's-Not – My-Style – No – Not-At-All

My-Style-Baby – Is-Getting-It-On
So-What – Do-You-Say – Baby
Do-You – Do-You – Do-You-Want-To
Rock My Bone

(Chorus)
Come On Baby – Rock My Bone
It's Such A Great Bone To Rock
Come On Baby – Rock My Bone
If You Say No – Baby
I'll Let Some Other Hottie
Fall In Love With – Rockin' My Bone
So Come On Baby – Rock My Bone
Before You Lose Your Chance
At Rockin' Along With The Perfect Bone

Book Six: Do You Remember Rock And Roll (Pages 4-36)

(Side One)
101. Rocking The World (579.)
102. Rock Seem Dead (173.)
    Rock Seem Dead (Flash-Back Demos)
103. It Don't Matter (171.)
104. Stain (181.)
    Stain (Second Staining Version)
105. Coming Home (214.)

(Side Two)
106. I Am The Rock (That Likes To Roll) (576.)
107. One Life, Rock On (506.)
    One Life, Rock On (Second Rocking Edition)
108. Two Crazy Lovers (328.)
109. Wrecking Ball (507.)
110. Freedom's Mountain (206.)

(Side Three)
111. Do You Remember Rock And Roll (118.)
112. Rock Is Good (Take Two) (581.)
113. Cave Man (129.)
114. Return To Hell (196.)
115. Your Canvas Is Your Soul (528.)

(Side Four)
    Rock And Roll House (73.) (Extra Bonus)
116. Rock And Roll House #2 (507 Songs Later) (580.)
117. I Write The Lyrics (Who Cares) (224.)
118. Flush It (You Stupid Stool Samples) (344.)
119. Bounty Hunter (146.)
120. Earth Prisoner (# Way Too Many) (185.)

(Bonus Songs)
Rock Is Good (Take One) (144.)
Rock Is Good (Take Three) (587.)

101. Rocking The World

I-Like to Rock and Roll
Have a Great-Time
Rocking and Rolling-Away
To-My – Dull-Life
It's all Good – All the Time
Especially – Making-Love

If-You – Want to Party
Just-Tell-Me – Where to Be
I'll-Be the Life of It
As-I – Rock and Roll
The-Crowded-House
All – Night – Long

(Chorus)
Rocking The World – Makes Me Feel Free
Rocking The World – Makes Me Stay Hard
Rocking The World – Is Really Good For Me
Come on World – Let-Me – Rock-You-Hard

Play-Some-Old-Favorites
Everybody – On-Their-Feet
Rocking and Rolling
Have a Great-Time
Rocking – Along with Me

If-You – Want to Party
Just-Tell-Me – Where to Be
I'll-Be the Life of It
As-I – Rock and Roll
The-Crowded-House
All – Night – Long

(Chorus)
Rocking The World – Makes Me Feel Free
Rocking The World – Makes Me Stay Hard
Rocking The World – Is Really Good For Me
Come On World – Let-Me – Rock-You-Hard

Come On World – Let-Me – Rock-You – Harder
Come On World – Let-Me – Rock-You – Even-Harder
Come On World – I'm-Just-Starting – To-Rock-You

5

102. Rock Seem Dead

Living-High – Party-Hard
Dance and Dance – Shake-Your-Ass
Coke it Up – Drink it Down
Such an Elegant-Party
Have a Great-Time
If-You-Need a Ride
Come-Over and Talk to Me-Later

What is Your-Name
Do-You-Plan to Party or Die-Tonight
Good-News – You-Will-Live – One-More-Night
Then-Again – I-Might be Lying

(Chorus)
Why The Hell Does
Rock Seem Dead
It Was Everywhere Once
Making This Planet Seem Better
I Don't Know About You
But I Sure As Hell – Miss It

Living-High – Party-Hard
Dance and Dance – Shake-Your-Ass
Coke it Up – Drink it Down
Such an Elegant-Party
Have a Great-Time
If-You-Need a Ride
Come-Over and Talk to Me-Later

What is Your-Name
Do-You-Plan to Party or Die-Tonight
Good-News – You-Will-Live – One-More-Night
Then-Again – I-Might be Lying

(Chorus)
Why The Hell Does
Rock Seem Dead
It Was Everywhere Once
Making This Planet Seem Better
I Don't Know About You
But I Sure As Hell – Miss It

Rock Seems Dead (Flash-Back Demos)

Flash-Back #1

Can-I – Ask-You-This
Why The Hell Does
Rock Seem Dead
It Was Everywhere Once
Making This Planet Seem Better
I Don't Know About You
But I Sure As Hell – Miss It

(Chorus)
Rock Seems Dead
Mother Earth Is Crying
Rock Seems Dead
All The People Are Dying
Rock Seems Dead
This Seems So Familiar
Rock Seems Dead
I Think I'm Having a Flash-Back

Flash-Back #2

Can-I – Ask-You-This
Why The Hell Does
Rock Seem Dead
It Was Everywhere Once
Making This Planet Seem Better
I Don't Know About You
But I Sure As Hell – Miss It

(Chorus)
Rock Seems Dead
Maybe It's All In My Mind
Rock Seems Dead
Maybe It's Not In My Mind
Rock Seems Dead
This Seems So Familiar
Rock Seems Dead
I Think I'm Having a Flash-Back

103. It Don't Matter

Get-Up in the Morning
Kick-My – Dreams-Away
Letting in the Heaviness
Readying-Myself to Be the Person
The-World-Expects – Me to Be

It's-Tiring as Hell
I've-Had – Enough of It
No-More – Doing it for Anybody
Time to Do-It for Myself
What-I-Want – What-I-Need

(Chorus)
It Don't Matter – If You Like Me
It Don't Matter
Because I Like Myself
It Don't Matter
What I Think – Is All That Matters
It Don't Matter – If You Agree Or Not

You-Don't – Know-Me
Still-You – Give-Me so Much-Hate
For-Not – Being-Your-Clone
You-Definitely – Eat-Out of the Crapper
For-Being this Way at Looking at Life

You're just Another – Pocket-Playing
Nothing-Happening – Wasting-Away
Person that is Too-Scared
To be Your – Own-Person
Hating-Me – Because-I'm-Not – Anymore

(Chorus)
It Don't Matter – If You Like Me
It Don't Matter
Because I Like Myself
It Don't Matter
What I Think – Is All That Matters
It Don't Matter – If You Agree Or Not

World-Been on My-Ass – Long-Enough
I'm-Wiping it Away
No – More – Damn – Streaks
It-Keeps on Trying to Give-Me

Freedom – I-Shout – Out-Loud
I'm-Doing – My-Thing
My-Corner of the World
Screams at Me – No-More
I'm-Grabbed – Tied-Up and Dragged-Away

(Chorus)
It Don't Matter – If You Like Me
It Don't Matter
Because I Like Myself
It Don't Matter
What I Think – Is All That Matters
It Don't Matter – If You Agree Or Not

The-Outcast is to Be-Made
To-Look – Like a Fool
Laughter in the Town-Circle
The-Outcast – Smiles without Fear
Waiting to Show these Haters
What-He is Made-Of

The-Best of Them – Are the Ones
That-Pull-Down – My-Pants
To-Their-Surprise – I'm-Streak-Free
The-Best – Let-Go and Back-Away
As-I – Turn-Around to Give-Out-Shock

Laughter-Turns to Silence – Silence-Turns to Praise
I-Stand-Proud – Showing-Off what Happens – When-You
Become – Your-Own-Person – Instead of a Clone

(Chorus)
It Don't Matter – If You Like Me
It Don't Matter
Because I Like Myself
It Don't Matter
What I Think – Is All That Matters
It Don't Matter – If You Agree Or Not

9

104. Stain

I'm-Not-You – You're-Not-Me
I'm-Me – The-One and Only
Why – Can't-You – See-This
You-Should – Know-Better
But-You – Never-Will

Always – Saying and Doing
What-You-Think is Best for Me
If-You – Want to Know
I'd be Glad to Tell-You
Just-What – I-Want and Need

(Chorus)
I'm The Stain
That Will Not Go Away
No Matter How Much
You Try To Scrub Me Off
I Will Remain Present
For The World To See

Since – I'm-Not – Like-You
Or – Believe in What – You-Do
I'm-Put-On – Your-Hate-List
Just-Another in the Way – Stain
That-You-Think – You-Can
Get-Rid-Of – Whenever-You-Want

This is a Fact – You-Fools
You will Never – Understand
I'm a Special-One
Just like Everybody-Else – You-Hate
You're too One-Minded
To-Open – Your-Hate-Filled-Eyes
To-See the Real-Truth

(Chorus)
I'm The Stain
That Will Not Go Away
No Matter How Much
You Try To Scrub Me Off
I Will Remain Present
For The World To See

Stain (Second Staining Version)

Look at Them – Over-There
I'm The Stain
Let's-Make-Them – Understand
That-They-Don't-Belong
I'm – The – Stain
That-Will-Not-Go-Away

Look at Her – Over-There
I'm – The – Stain
She' so Hot – She's a Yes for Sure
She-Better say Yes to Me
I'm – The – Stain
That-Will-Not-Go-Away

(Chorus)
I'm The Stain
That Will Not Go Away
No Matter How Much
You Try To Scrub Me Off
I Will Remain Present
For The World To See

Look at All that Blood
I'm The Stain
How-Many – Were-Killed this Time
I can't Believe – This Keeps Going-On
I'm – The – Stain
That-Will-Not-Go-Away

(Chorus)
I'm The Stain
That Will Not Go Away
No Matter How Much
You Try To Scrub Me Off
I Will Remain Present
For The World To See

I-Hear-Next-Week – There's a Chance
For a Nuclear-Holocaust
I'm – The – Stain
That-Will-Be-Here – Forever and a Day

11

105. Coming Home

The-Road-Tries to Own-You
Makes-You – Feel it Everyday
It's-Your – Endless-Torment
Your – Second – Home

Misery – Loves – Company
This-Band's – Been-Together
For so Many – Long-Years
Living and Taking it All-In
Being the Rock and Roll-Idols
For-Our – Millions of Fans

(Chorus)
I'm Coming Home
I've Been Away Too Long
I Can't Wait To See
Your Beautiful Face
And Your Sweet-Sexy Smile

On-The-Road – You-Have to Keep
Yourself and Your-Mind – Busy
Or – You-Can-Take the Chance
Letting-What-May-Come – Come-Your-Way
It's so Easy to Give-In
Temptation-Follows-You – Everywhere

You-Can – Turn-Your-Head
Ignoring – Yourself
As-You-Feel – That-Rush
Making it So-Easy for You to Go-On
Erasing the Pain of The-Road
Replacing it With – Rock-God-Ness

(Chorus)
I'm Coming Home
I've Been Away Too Long
I Can't Wait To See
Your Beautiful Face
And Your Sweet-Sexy Smile

Everybody-Makes-Mistakes
Rock and Rollers Have More
Time on Their-Hands
To – Make – Them – And
More-Money to Spend-On – Them

Take it From-Me – You-Can
Kick-Some-Rock and Roll – Ass
Or – You-Can-Let – Rock and Roll
Kick-Your-Ass – Riding-Down the Road

(Chorus)
I'm Coming Home
I've Been Away Too Long
I Can't Wait To See
Your Beautiful Face
And Your Sweet-Sexy Smile

It-Takes-Years of Hard-Work
And – Dedication to Make-It
If-You're – Great-Enough
Dreams – Sometimes-Do – Come-True
When-You-Get-Your-Shot
Live-It to Its-Fullest

For it's Your – Rock and Roll Dream
If-You – Can-Live it Clean
Then-Maybe it Won't – Turn-Out to Be
Your – Rock and Roll – Nightmare

(Chorus)
I'm Coming Home
I've Been Away Too Long
I Can't Wait To See
Your Beautiful Face
And Your Sweet-Sexy Smile

106. I Am The Rock (That Likes To Roll)

I-Have-Returned
Been-Away too Long
Now that I'm-Back
You Know – What that Means
Rock and Roll

I'm the Love in Your-Heart
That-You've – Been-Missing
Time's-Made-Me – Hard to Remember
But-I will Never be Forgotten
Because – Rock and Roll
Will – Never – Die

(Chorus)
I Am The Rock
That Likes To Roll
I'm In Every One Of You
Let's Make Our Lives
One Big Party Again
Rocking And Rolling
Away Our Blues

The-Festival has Started
People-Having a Good-Time
Rocking and Rolling
Forgetting the Pains
That-Their-Lives – Brings to Them

Good-Food – Good-Drink – Good-Times
Everybody is Partying
Hate and Loneliness are On-Pause
As the Winds of Change
Come-Rocking and Rolling-By

(Chorus)
I Am The Rock
That Likes To Roll
I'm In Every One Of You
Let's Make Our Lives
One Big Party Again
Rocking And Rolling
Away Our Blues
14

107. One Life Rock On

People that I've-Known for Years
Looks-Like – They-All – Have a Room
In the Ready for Their-Ending
Not-Me – My-Mind's on Fire
I'm-Ready for Some-More – New-Life
Even if I-Have to Make it Become
A-Reality – All by Myself

(Chorus)
One Life, Rock On
Waiting Is For Settling
One Life, Rock On
Lying Down On The Ground
Is For When I'm Dying
One Life, Rock On
I Ain't Ready To Die Yet

Felt-Myself-Slipping – My-Mind
Started-Down a Downward – Spiral
My-Youth was Dying – I'm-Crying-Inside
So-Damn-Cold – I've-Sunken-Over
Looking – Into the Mirror – I-Hate the One
I'm-Looking-At – Don't-Wanna – Rip-His-Face-Off
For-All-I-Wanna-Do is Smile

(Chorus)
One Life, Rock On
Waiting Is For Settling
One Life, Rock On
Lying Down On The Ground
Is For When I'm Dying
One Life, Rock On
I Ain't Ready To Die Yet

Walking the Years-Away – My-Mind is Clearing
I'm-Living-Free – One-Day at a Time
No-More-Damn-Heavy on My-Back
Where-I-Stop – Nobody-Knows-Me
I-Slide-In for a Few-Moments
Keeping-My-Humanity – Charging-Bright

(Repeat Chorus)

One Life, Rock On (Second Rocking Edition)

Silence – My-Mind is Ticking
Heartbreaking – My-Life is Half-Way-Over
Ain't-That-Sad – What-Can-I-Do – About-It
Get-Up – Get-Myself-Moving
Rock and Roll

(Chorus)
One Life, Rock On
Waiting Is For Settling
One Life, Rock On
Lying Down On The Ground
Is For When I'm Dying
One Life, Rock On
I Ain't Ready To Die Yet

Yesterday – What a Scream
One-Day – Turned into Twenty-Years
Ain't-That-Sad – What-Can-I-Do – About-It
Get-Up – Get-Myself-Moving
Rock and Roll

(Chorus)
One Life, Rock On
Waiting Is For Settling
One Life, Rock On
Lying Down On The Ground
Is For When I'm Dying
One Life, Rock On
I Ain't Ready To Die Yet

Tomorrow – I-Don't-Know
And-I-Don't-Care – Rock-On
Ain't-That-Great – What-Can-I-Do – About-It
I'll-Tell-You-What
I'll-Keep-On-Living – Each-Day – Like it's My-Last
Rock and Roll

(Repeat Chorus)

16

108. Two Crazy Lovers

Jamie and Jimmy are Not-Normal
They-Live their Lives – Differently
They-Love – Each-Other
But – They're – Desperate
They have No- Jobs and No-Home
All-They-Do is Drive-Around
Town to town – Looking for a John to Roll

Someone – That is Lonely-Enough
To-Take – Jamie-Home for the Night
They-Get – What-They-Want
When-John – Can't go No more
When – Getting-Up – Seems-Like-Work
Jimmy-Comes-In to Tie-Up-John

(Chorus)
Two Crazy Lovers
Jamie Picks Up A John
Has Sex With Him – Until He Can't Move
Then Jimmy Comes In – And Knocks Out John
Then The Two Crazy Lover – Robs John Blind

Jamie – I-Love-You – This-Can't –Go-On
Jimmy – I-Love-You – What-Choice do We-Have
Jamie-I'll-Get a Job – We'll-Buy a House
Dream-On Jimmy – I-Love-My-Life
Jamie-I-Love-You – I-Said-No more-Johns
Jimmy-I-Love-You – But-Your-Starting to Piss-Me-Off

Jamie-It's-Me or Them / Jimmy-Pull-Over – I'm-Driving-Now
Jamie – I-Love-You – Please-Unlock the Door
Jimmy – I-Don't-Love-You – You-Lack in the Sack
Jamie-I-Think – All-Those-John's – Turned-You into a Slut
Jimmy – You-Better-Run – Before-I-Turn-You into Road-Kill
Jamie-You're-One – Crazy-Bitch-Lover / Rock-You-Jimmy

(Chorus)
Two Crazy Lovers
Jamie Picks Up A John
Has Sex With Him – Until He Can't Move
Then Jimmy Comes In – And Knocks Out John
Then The Two Crazy Lover – Robs John Blind

109. Wrecking Ball

Walking the Streets
Selling – Your-Everything
Getting those Dollars
That-Make-You – Bleed-Inside

Scarred and Damned
You're in a Living-Hell
Watching-Empty – Very-Crazed
Hate-Filled-Eyes – Having-Their – Paid-Dollars
All-Over-Your – Numbed-Body

(Chorus)
Wrecking Ball – I'm Your
Damn Wrecking Ball
Ready To Destroy
Your Damned Life
You're All Messed Up
And You Don't Care
I'm So Glad To Be Your
Needed Wreaking Ball

Walking-Away from Your-Fans
You-Need a Few-Moments
Sweating – Getting-Hot – Hating-It
Time-Limit is Up – On-Your-Fix

Gotta-Jam that Needle-In
Feel that Pure-Refreshing – Blast
You're-Back on Your-Feet
Ready to Be the One-Again
Everybody – Aspires to Be-Like

(Chorus)
Wrecking Ball – I'm Your
Damn Wrecking Ball
Ready To Destroy
Your Damned Life
You're All Messed Up
And You Don't Care
I'm So Glad To Be Your
Needed Wreaking Ball

18

You-Can't-Take it Any-More
Your-World is So-Dirty
No-More – Beauty-Anywhere
Everybody is Doing-It
Why-Shouldn't – You-Do it Too

Bring-On the Pain
Bring-On Death
Your-Time to Shine-Bright
Is for the Having
Jump and Do-Your – Worst

(Chorus)
Wrecking Ball – I'm Your
Damn Wrecking Ball
Ready To Destroy
Your Damned Life
You're All Messed Up
And You Don't Care
I'm So Glad To Be Your
Needed Wreaking Ball

Bullets-Spraying
Bloody-Penetrating
You're-Blown-Away
Dead on the Ground
Marked-Another-Crazy
Mad-Killing-Monster
From-Hostile-Breeding
And – Poor-Living-Conditions

(Chorus)
Wrecking Ball – I'm Your
Damn Wrecking Ball
Ready To Destroy
Your Damned Life
You're All Messed Up
And You Don't Care
I'm So Glad To Be Your
Needed Wreaking Ball

110. Freedom's Mountain

I'm so Burnt-Out – Have to Get-Away
Take a Break from My-Life
That's-Become a Living-Hell
Forced to Do the Same-Thing
Day-After-Day for So-Long

I-Don't-Know – What-Anymore
Feels-Like – I'm-Here – Just to
Keep-Going – On and On
Like-I'm-Never – Allowed to Stop
Doing it All for Work
Forgetting – All-About-Myself

(Chorus)
I'm Climbing Up So Very High
This Is Exactly What I Need
I'm Going To Climb To The Top
Setting Myself Free On Top Of
Freedom's Mountain

My-World is Slowly-Calming
As-I-Drive – Towards-Freedom
Never-Been this Way – Before
Never-Done-Anything – Like this Before
I'm-Totally-Alone for the First-Time
Loving that I'm-Letting-Myself – Have-This

Don't-Know for Sure – If-I-Can – Do-This
And – I – Don't – Care – Right – Now
I'm-Doing-This – Nothing's – Gonna-Stop-Me
I-Have to Break – Through the Barriers
I-Let the World – Make-Out of My-Life

(Chorus)
I'm Climbing Up So Very High
This Is Exactly What I Need
I'm Going To Climb To The Top
Setting Myself Free On Top Of
Freedom's Mountain

Standing at the Bottom of Beautiful
Looking-Up to the Top – Where-My-Journey will End
Breathing in Nature's – Wonderful-Clean-Air
I'm-Ready to Take – My-Feet – Forward and Up
Ready to Make – My-Body-Ache – For its Freedom

My-Stiff and Tired-Body is Crying-Out for Me to Stop
My-Mind is On-Fire – Thinking-Clearly at Last
With-Each – Painful-Pull-Upwards – More-Clarity is Rising
My-Body-May-Feel – Like-Giving-Up – Already in Defeat
But-My-Becoming – Stronger-Mind – Won't-Let-It

(Chorus)
I'm Climbing Up So Very High
This Is Exactly What I Need
I'm Going To Climb To The Top
Setting Myself Free On Top Of
Freedom's Mountain

Reaching the Top of Freedom's-Mountain
My-Mind is Completely-Clear – For the First-Time
I-Open-Up – My-Backpack – Bringing-Out a Candle

Lighting-Up the Candle – Tears-Fall from My-Eyes
For the Long – Lost-Life – I was Forced – Not to Live – and
To the New-Free-Life – That-I-Will be Living – From-Now-On

(Chorus)
I'm Climbing Up So Very High
This Is Exactly What I Need
I'm Going To Climb To The Top
Setting Myself Free On Top Of
Freedom's Mountain

(Chorus)
I'm Climbing Up So Very High
This Is Exactly What I Need
I'm Going To Climb To The Top
Setting Myself Free On Top Of
Freedom's Mountain

111. Do You Remember Rock And Roll

Yesterday was No-Dream – Come-True
Belly of the Beast is Never – Full
Snow-Falls-Down – Gray
Love is Still-Not- Forever
And-I – Lost-My-Sweater

As-I-Stand-Here – Shivering
Wearing-Only – My-Pants
Like a Stranger – I-Ask-Myself-This

(Chorus)
Do You Remember Rock And Roll
And What It Did
For You And Your Soul
It Kept You Young – Free And Hard
So Come Back To Rock
Start Rocking And Rolling Again

No-Whispers in the Wind
No-Calm of the Storm
I'm-Alone in This-World
Rock and Roll – Will be My-Friend
While-Peace and Harmony is My-Destination

Over the Hill and Down the Other-Side
Is a Man – Wearing-My-Sweater
Who-Has – No-Pants
So-I-Ask – This-Stranger-This

(Chorus)
Do You Remember Rock And Roll
And What It Did
For You And Your Soul
It Kept You Young – Free And Hard
So Come Back To Rock
Start Rocking And Rolling Again

112. Rock Is Good (Take Two)

Hey-Ladies – Hey-Dudes
Hate and Fear's – Time is Here
I-Say – Hell with That
Time to Rock – These-Heavies
Down the Freaking-Drain

You-Have the Right to Be-Down
Frustrated – Bored and Angry
It's-Your-Life – Live it Free
All-I'm-Saying – There's
Another Side and Way
If-You-Want to Check it Out
It – Goes – Like – This

(Chorus)
Rock Is Good
Rock Is Great
Add It To Your Life
So You Can Rock Your Ass Off
Before You Die From Boredom

Welcome to the Party
Look-Around at All the People
Life is Happening this Moment
All the Different-People
Came to Have a Good-Time

Rock – Sex and Freedom
Is-Being – Served-Up-Tonight
All-New – Fresh and Tasty
So-Stop-Watching and Wanting
Jump-Your – Non-Rocking Ass
Into the Safe-Flames of Rock and Roll

(Chorus)
Rock Is Good
Rock Is Great
Add It To Your Life
So You Can Rock Your Ass Off
Before You Die From Boredom

113. Cave Man

I-Don't-Know-Enough or Care to
Just so I-Can – Impress-You
Being-Like-You – Want-Me to Be
Makes – No-Sense at All

All the Talking and Yelling
Does-No-Good – I just Look at You
Pushing-Me-Around and Bullying-Me
Only-Makes-Me-Angry
Wanting to Get-Away from You
For-You're an Angry-Animal

(Chorus)
I Am – A Cave Man / You Stupid Animal
I Am – A Cave Man / Leave Me Alone
I Am – A Cave Man / I Do Not Want – To Be Like You
I Am – A Cave Man / Just Leave Me In Peace

You-Dress-Me-Up – Similar to You
Getting-Me to Repeat – Words like
Government and Conform
Pat-Me on My-Head
When-I-Start to Understand

Agreeing with Everything – You-Say
You-Get-Me – Out-There
Doing – What – You – Want
Making-Me-Make – Others-Like-Me
Do the Same-Things – You-Want

(Chorus)
I Am – A Cave Man / You Stupid Animal
I Am – A Cave Man / Leave Me Alone
I Am – A Cave Man / I Do Not Want – To Be Like You
I Am – A Cave Man / Just Leave Me In Peace

Man-Do-I-Miss the Cave-Life
It was so Simple – Living-Together
We-Knew-One-Kind of Cave-Man
Could-Not-Be the Way for survival
In a World – So-Filled-Up
With-So-Many – Different-Kinds of Life

24

114. Return To Hell

I-Have – Hardly-Anything
The-Man just Loves-This
So-What if I'm-Free
What the Hell is This
Doing – For – Me
Nothing and Extra-Thick at That
Making-My-Mind – Pound with Fear

I'm just Another – Ordinary
This-World-Created – Born-Only
To-Comply – Cast-Out – When-I-Don't
Large-Glass of Mind-Taking – Wine
To go Along-With the Free-Meal
I-Get – When-My-Comply is Refreshed
Ready to Beat in Union
Me and The-Man – Hand and Hand

(Chorus)
Out For Myself This Time
Running Away As Fast As I Can
Nothing Gonna Stop Me
Nothing Gonna Bring Me Back
So I Can Return To Hell

Hey-Man – Listen-Up – You're-Doing-Bad
Do the Good-Thing – Protect-Our-Rights
Get-Together and Do-What is Best
Hell with Your-Endless – Bickering

Men and Women of This-Country
Make it Beautiful – However-Man
We don't Feel – Any-Love – Coming from You
All of You – Are-Only-There to Do for Us
Not to Run – Our-Lives – That is Ours-Forever

(Chorus)
Out For Myself This Time
Running Away As Fast As I Can
Nothing Gonna Stop Me
Nothing Gonna Bring Me Back
So I Can Return To Hell

Only-Thing – Can-Be is This
We have Way too Many – Poor-People
That-Can-Not – Afford-Extra for You
Pass a Bill that Lets-Us – Pay what We-Can – Afford
Not what You-Think – We-Should-Pay
It is Doomed to Fail – For like We-Said
We-Do-Not – Have it For-You to Make it Work

Elections – Elections are Coming-Up
We the People – Want-Our just Rewards
So-Sad – What-You did Man – Uncaring-Man
You Made this Country-Bleed

(Chorus)
Out For Myself This Time
Running Away As Fast As I Can
Nothing Gonna Stop Me
Nothing Gonna Bring Me Back
So I Can Return To Hell

I'm-Taking – My-Stand
I-Hate – Hate – I -Love – Love
I'm-No-Way-Perfect
I'm in Constant-Battle to Ascend
To be much Better than I-Am

I-Want-My – Tomorrow-Now
I'm-Real-Tired of Waiting for It
How-About-All-You – We the People
Have-You – Finally-Woke – Your-Asses-Up
Or are You Just Gonna – Sit-There and
Eat – Crap and Repeat – Forevermore

(Chorus)
Out For Myself This Time
Running Away As Fast As I Can
Nothing Gonna Stop Me
Nothing Gonna Bring Me Back
So I Can Return To Hell

115. Your Canvas Is Your Soul

Paint-Me a Picture
Full of the Love – In-Your-Heart
Add the Pain of Your-Day
Watch as it Becomes a Reflection

Bring-Forth the Lust and Hate
That-Exists in Everybody's
Cold and Lonely-World
It is Now – Alive

(Chorus)
Your Canvas Is Your Soul
Do You Want It To Smile
Your Canvas Is Your Soul
Do You Want It To Scream
Your Canvas Is Your Soul
It Is All Up To You

The-Good and The-Bad
All-Walk-Around – Together
Along-With the Lonely
And the Not-Satisfied
Nobody's the Same

Being-Different is Not a Sin
Life is a Discovery – Waiting to Happen
Everyday does Not – Have to Be the Same

(Chorus)
Your Canvas Is Your Soul
Do You Want It To Smile
Your Canvas Is Your Soul
Do You Want It To Scream
Your Canvas Is Your Soul
It Is All Up To You

Life will Go-On and so Will-Time
While-You're-Trying to Make-Up – Your-Mind
Rather-You-Want to Live-Life to its Fullest
Or – Kick-Back and Let it Pass-You-By

(Repeat Chorus)
27

Rock And Roll House (73.) (Extra Bonus)

Work-Week is Over
Damn it Was a Long-One
Let the Weekend – Begin
Start this Friday-Night – Up just Right
Time for Beer – Women and Song

(Chorus)
Rock
Rock
Rock And Roll House
Rock
Rock
It's A Rock And Roll House

Partying-Hearty – Real-Hard
Just – Rocking – Away
Having a Great-Time
Jamming – Holding-My-Beer
I-Have a Rocking – Good-Buzz – Going-On

(Chorus)
Rock
Rock
Rock And Roll House
Rock
Rock
It's A Rock And Roll House

She-Sits on My-Lap
Gets-Me – Real-Hard – Real-Quick
She-Likes – What-She-Feels
It is Time to Find a Bedroom
Looking-Forward to Pounding – My-Buzz-Away

(Chorus)
Rock
Rock
Rock And Roll House
Rock
Rock
It's A Rock And Roll House

28

116. Rock And Roll House #2 (507 Songs Later)

It's – Friday – Night
It's-Time to Find a Party-Hardy
Drinking some Beer – Find some Sweet-Tail
Rock – And – Roll
Let – Me – Make a Call

(Chorus)
Rock-Rock – Rock And Roll House
Rock-Rock – It's a Rock And Roll House
Rock-Rock – Rock And Roll House
Rock-Rock – It's a Rock And Roll House

Great – Damn – News
There's a Huge – Party-Tonight
At the Rock and Roll-House
So-Get-Off – Your-Sitting-Ass
Come-Along with Me
'Cause-I-Need to Do – Some-Rockin'
And-You-Got – Nothing-Better to Do

(Chorus)
Rock-Rock – Rock And Roll House
Rock-Rock – It's a Rock And Roll House
Rock-Rock – Rock And Roll House
Rock-Rock – It's a Rock And Roll House

Look at All the Ladies here Tonight
Dressed-Up and Looking so Fine
Bringing-Their – Sweet-Honey-Scents
To-Add to All the Brew
That is Being-Poured-Out – Tonight

Going to Drink – One more Down
Then-Find-Myself the Best-Piece of Tail
That-I-Can – Rock and Roll – With

(Chorus)
Rock-Rock – Rock And Roll House
Rock-Rock – It's a Rock And Roll House
Rock-Rock – Rock And Roll House
Rock-Rock – It's a Rock And Roll House

29

117. I Write The Lyrics (Who Cares)

I-Write the Lyrics that Make-You-Happy
I-Write the Lyrics that Make-You – Want to Love
I-Write the Lyrics that -You – Want to Live
I-Write the Lyrics that Make-You – Love-Life

I-Write the Lyrics that Make-You so Sad
I-Write the Lyrics that Make-You – Want to Cry
I-Write the Lyrics that Make-You – Crazy
I-Write the Lyrics that Make-You – Sane

(Chorus)
Who Cares It Don't Matter
Keep It To Yourself
Who Cares It Don't Matter
What The Hell You Wrote
Who Cares It Don't Matter
Shut The Hell Up
Who Cares What Only Matters
Is What You Do Next

I-Write the Lyrics that You-Love to Love
I-Write the Lyrics that You-Hate to Hate
I-Write the Lyrics that You-Hate to Love
I-Write the Lyrics that You-Love to Hate

I-Write the Lyrics that Drive-You – Wild
I-Write the Lyrics that You-Want to Go-Away
I-Write the Lyrics that Make-You – Horny
I-Write the Lyrics that You-Want to Destroy

(Chorus)
Who Cares It Don't Matter
Keep It To Yourself
Who Cares It Don't Matter
What The Hell You Wrote
Who Cares It Don't Matter
Shut The Hell Up
Who Cares What Only Matters
Is What You Do Next

118. Flush It (You Stupid Stool Samples)

All the Time – Everywhere
All there Seems to Be
Out and About at Night
Are a Bunch of Crap – Talking-People
That-Don't-Know-Anything
But-How to Crap on Your-Night

I-Know – I-Don't-Know it All
Never -Claimed to Be – One-Either
Maybe it's Just-Me but All
Crap-Talkers All at the Same-Time
Seem to Have – Stank-Breath
Making-Me – Say to Them

(Chorus)
Flush It – You Stupid Stool Samples
You're Suppose To Flush It
Not Chew And Eat It
So Flush It – Flush It
You Nasty Talking – Crap-Filled People

All the Time – Everywhere
All there Seems to Be
Out and About at Night
Are a Bunch of Hate – Talking-People
That-Don't-Know-Anything
But-How to Hate-Fill – Your-Night

I-Know – I'm-No-Saint
Never-Claimed to Be – One-Either
Maybe it's Just-Me but All
Hate-Talkers – All at the Same-Time
Seem to Have – Stank-Breath
Making-Me – Say to Them

(Chorus)
Flush It – You Stupid Stool Samples
You're Suppose To Flush It
Not Chew And Eat It
So Flush It – Flush It
You Nasty Talking – Crap-Filled People

119. Bounty Hunter

Out in the Cold – Dark-Night
Is-Nothing to Me
Gladly-Brave – All-Elements
Staying – Out of Eye-Sight
Ready to Grab-You-Up

Waiting 'til You-Show
Might seem Boring to Some
It's so Easy for Me
I-Turn – Myself-Off – And
Bring-Out the Bounty-Hunter

(Chorus)
I-Don't-Care – If You're Innocent Or Guilty
Only Thing That Matters
Is The Price On Your Head
Fighting Or Fleeing – Will Do You – No Good
Accept Your Fate – Give Up
Bow To The Bounty Hunter

Take-You in Alive
Or – Bloody-Dumb-Dead
Is an End to a Means
Another – Meal – Ticket
Out-There – Ready to Be – Cashed-In

On the Run – Nothing to Lose
Makes-My-Prey – Do some Stupid-Things
Like-Trying to Out-Fight-Me
Damn-Fools – I am Strong from Catching
So-Many of You – For so Long

(Chorus)
I-Don't-Care – If You're Innocent Or Guilty
Only Thing That Matters
Is The Price On Your Head
Fighting Or Fleeing – Will Do You – No Good
Accept Your Fate – Give Up
Bow To The Bounty Hunter

My-Work is Lonely
If-I-Think – About-It – So-I-Don't
Hit the Bars – Hit the Clubs
Find-Myself – Something-I-Want and Need
This-World is Full of Things
That a Man – Like-Me-Wants

Women – So-Many of Them – Are
In-Waiting – For a Hard-Life – Bad-Man
Willing to Give-Them the Night
They-Will – Never-Forget

(Chorus)
I-Don't-Care – If You're Innocent Or Guilty
Only Thing That Matters
Is The Price On Your Head
Fighting Or Fleeing – Will Do You – No Good
Accept Your Fate – Give Up
Bow To The Bounty Hunter

Hell – If-I-Really – Feel-Like – Getting-It-On
I-Let-One of My – Fine-Ladies – Come-Along
They-Watch as I – Grab-You-Up
They-Pant – When-I-Tie-You-Up
They-Moan – When-I-Throw-You in the Trunk

Always the Look of Anything
I-Want in Their-Eyes and This
Bad-Ass – Bounty-Hunter – Likes-That
Wipe-Your-Blood – Off-My-Hands
Turn-You-In – Cash-My-Check
Then-Jump – Straight-Into the Sack

(Chorus)
I-Don't-Care – If You're Innocent Or Guilty
Only Thing That Matters
Is The Price On Your Head
Fighting Or Fleeing – Will Do You – No Good
Accept Your Fate – Give Up
Bow To The Bounty Hunter

120. Earth Prisoner (# Way Too Many)

I was Just a Galaxy-Playboy
Rich-Kid that Had-Looks
Which-Got-Me
Lots and Lots of Fine-Ladies

Only to Get a Hold of the Wrong-One
The-Minister's – Only-Daughter
Which – Got – Me – Kicked-Forever
The Hell off Their
Not-Having – My-Kind of Person
On-Their-Kind Of Planet – Ever-Again

(Chorus)
Life Is Not Fair – My Planet Sucks
Earth Is Cool – The Beer and Weed Are Great
Only Damn Problem Is
I'm Earth Prisoner (# Way Too Many)
With No Way Of Ever Going Back Home Again
My Planet Sucks – I'm Going To Make Them Pay
It's Time – I Tell The Humans What's Going On

From-Getting-Laid – All the Time
To-Stuck on Earth – Horny with Two-Free – Hands
Not-My-Life-Style – Earth-Ladies will Do just Fine
Cost of My-Rebellion is High

Knock at My-Door – Damn-Galaxy-Police
Whip-My-Ass – Telling-Me – I-Should have Said-No
All-My-Fault – I-Own-My-Pain – Such a Drag
Life is a Privilege when Your a Earth-Prisoner

Never-Forget to Thank – The-Damn-Galaxy-Police
For the Ass-Whipping that Put-You – Back in Your-Place

(Chorus)
Life Is Not Fair – My Planet Sucks
Earth Is Cool – The Beer and Weed Are Great
Only Damn Problem Is
I'm Earth Prisoner (# Way Too Many)
With No Way Of Ever Going Back Home Again
My Planet Sucks – I'm Going To Make Them Pay
It's Time – I Tell The Humans What's Going On
34

(Bonus Song)
Rock Is Good (Take One) (144.)

The-70's – Was a Great-Time
Being a Kid – My-Mind – Opened-Up to Rock
(Rock is Good – Rock is Great)

Record-Shop – Better than a Toy-Store
Listen to the Older-Kids – What-Jams – What-Rocks
(Rock is Good – Rock is Great)

Am-Stations – Playing-Singable-Song after Singable-Song
Fm-Stations – Playing-Rock – You-Can-Feel
(Life is too Short – I-Want to Be a Rock-Star)

Sing – This – With – Me

(Chorus)
Rock Is Good
Rock Is Great
When I Die
Play It At My Funeral
Send Me Off A-Rocking

The-80's – Gave-Me-Metal to Bang-My-Head
While-Driving-Around – Looking to Get-Laid
(Rock is Good – Rock is Great)

Now-I'm-Old – Ain't that Sick
One-Foot in a Grave – One-Foot on a Banana-Peel
(Rock is Good – Rock is Great)

Now-I'm a Ghost – Waiting on My-Funeral
Angel of Light – Angel of Dark – Who-Knows
(Life is too Short – I-Want to Be a Rock-Star)

Sing – This – With – Me

(Chorus)
Rock Is Good
Rock Is Great
When I Die
Play It At My Funeral
Send Me Off A-Rocking
35

(Bonus Song)
Rock Is Good (Take Three) (587.)

When the Pain of the Day
Shows on My-Face
When it Starts to Echo – Sameness
Deep-Into – My-Being
Making-Me – Want to Give-Up

I-Pick-My-Ass-Up
Put a Tune in My-Mind
Let this Tune – Come to Life
When-I-Pull – Out a 12-Inch – Record
Jamming it for Heaven – Jamming it for Hell

(Chorus)
Rock Is Good – Rock Is Great
When I Die – Add It To Your Life
Rock Is Good – Rock Is Great
Play It At My Funeral – So You Can Rock Your Ass Off
Rock Is Good – Rock Is Great
Send Me Off Rocking – Before You Die From Boredom

Day after Day – Life is Great
I-Rock and Roll – Hard and High
Just to Have a Great-Time
Day after Day – Life is Crap
I-Rock and Roll – Hard and High
Just to Find – Some-Damn – Peace of Mind

Loneliness and Anger – I-Try to Starve
Togetherness and Happiness – I-Try to Over-Feed
Doesn't-Always-Work & I-Don't-Care
One-Life – Rock-On – One-Life – Rock-On
I'll-Repeat this Freely – 'Til-My-Body – Feeds the Clay

(Chorus)
Rock Is Good – Rock Is Great
When I Die – Add It To Your Life
Rock Is Good – Rock Is Great
Play It At My Funeral – So You Can Rock Your Ass Off
Rock Is Good – Rock Is Great
Send Me Off Rocking – Before You Die From Boredom

36

Book Seven: Rock And Roll Bachelor (Pages 37-71)

(Side One)
121. Rock And Roll Bachelor (314.)
122. One More Time (315.)
123. Let's Love Shack Together (467.)
124. The Other (216.)
125. Give Her What I Promised (353.)

(Side Two)
126. Humping (410.)
127. I'm Cursed (411.)
128. Love Has Become A Four Letter Word (386.)
129. Let's Up And Down Together (529.)
130. So I Broke Your Heart (566.)

(Side Three)
131. The Push That Got Away (168.)
132. 6 + 1 = 7 Days In A Row (476.)
133. Don't Worry I Haven't Changed (519.)
134. Sparkless (459.)
135. Roar Out Your Hell (252.)

(Side Four)
  I Remember Rock And Roll (906.) (Extra Bonus)
136. Rocking & Rolling (205.)
  Rocking & Rolling (Second Rocking Version)
137. Dancing Sexsation (524.)
  Dancing Sexsation (First Dance Remix)
138. Love Is Too Slow (To Ever Catch Me) (257.)
139. The Death Of My Package (405.)
140. Blind Date #1 (183.)

(Bonus Songs)
Horny Animal Man (13.)
Too Damn Ugly To Get One (298.)

121. Rock And Roll Bachelor

Hello-Ladies – I'm-Here –Your
Rock and Roll Bachelor
Ready to Have a Great-Time
With a Bunch of Fine-Ladies
That-Have – No-Problem
Waiting for Their-Turn

So-Lick-Your-Lips
While-Shaking – Your-Hips
The-Lady with the Best-Ass
Gets to Be – Pleased-First

(Chorus)
Work Hard – Party Harder
Sleep A Little Bit
Eat When I Have The Time
I'm The Ready For Anything
And Can Go Anytime
Rock And Roll Bachelor
Come Rock And Roll With Me

Being the Longest-Best
Is-Easy – On-My – Happy-Soul
Knowing – That-I-Provide
Such-Good – Good – Lovin'
To so Many-Fine – Fine – Ladies
Almost-Brings – Tears to My-Eyes

But-I'm the Rock and Roll – Bachelor
Only-Tears that I-Ever-See
Are-From the Sweet-Ladies – That-Make-Them
After-I've – Pleased-Them – Passionately
Leaving-Them-Alone for the Next-One in Line

(Chorus)
Work Hard – Party Harder
Sleep A Little Bit
Eat When I Have The Time
I'm The Ready For Anything
And Can Go Anytime
Rock And Roll Bachelor
Come Rock And Roll With Me
38

122. One More Time

Come – Sit on My-Lap
Pretty – Tempting – Lover
You-Look so Sweet
I'd-Like a Taste of Your – Sexy-Style

That's it Hot-Lover – You-Take-Control
Go-Ahead – Sexy-Lady
Taste – My – Lips
As-I – Pull-You-In – Real-Close
To-Receive – Your-Special – Kiss

(Chorus)
Go Ahead Sexy Lover
Take Off Your Clothes
Show Me What You Got
Go Ahead Sexy Lover
Pull My Hair / Bite And Scratch Me
Go Ahead Sexy Lover
Let Out Your Moan / Then Tell Me
To Do It To You / One More Time

Hot-Lover that's Full of Desire
It's-Time for You to Explode
Smiling – Looking at You
Knowing – That-Proudly
I-Did-It – Again – So-Perfectly

Bless-Me for I-Have – Sinned
I'm so Full of Passion
I-Don't – Even-Mind – Damning
This-Hot-Lover – That-I'm – Playing-With

(Chorus)
Go Ahead Sexy Lover
Take Off Your Clothes
Show Me What You Got
Go Ahead Sexy Lover
Pull My Hair / Bite And Scratch Me
Go Ahead Sexy Lover
Let Out Your Moan / Then Tell Me
To Do It To You / One More Time

123. Let's Love Shack Together

Our-Smiles are Growing
While-Our – Nights-Together
Have-Turned-Out to Be
Something – We-Both-Love

Lust is In the Air – As-We
Never-Say those Magic-Words
We-Both – Feel so Deep
It-Shines on Our-Faces
That-We're into Something-Special

(Chorus)
Lover Of Mine
Smile If You Lust Me
I'm Right Here Right Now
Ready To Stay In Lust With You
I've Never Had Any Better
So-Lover – I'm-Thinking
Let's Love Shack Together

You-Smile at Me so Lovely
Telling-Me-That – You-Like-My (Pause)
It's-My-Best-Feature
Your – Personal – Favorite

I-Can-See in Your-Eyes
Those – Magic – Words
Are-Either-Hidden
Or – Not-There at All
I-Have to Know for Sure

(Chorus)
Lover Of Mine
Smile If You Lust Me
I'm Right Here Right Now
Ready To Stay In Lust With You
I've Never Had Any Better
So-Lover – I'm-Thinking
Let's Love Shack Together

I-Hand-You a Key to My-Pad
Stay with Me for Awhile
Find-Out if We-Love – Each Other
As-We-Turn-My-Pad
Into-Our – Very-Own – Love-Shack

We're-Shacked-Up – Real-Nice
Our-Lust is Very-Long – Lasting
Every – Single – Night
Don't-Want-This to End
So-I-Get-All – Big-Hearted
Asking-You to Marry-Me

(Chorus)
Lover Of Mine
Smile If You Lust Me
I'm Right Here Right Now
Ready To Stay In Lust With You
I've Never Had Any Better
So-Lover – I'm-Thinking
Let's Love Shack Together

With a Frown on Your-Face
With-Sadness in Your-Eyes
You-Tell-Me – No
Saying-That – I'm-Not the
Marrying-Type of Man

But-On the Plus-Side
My-Long-Hours of Lusting
Is-Enough for Staying
So-I-Say – Forget-It
Let's-Just-Keep-On
Love-Shacking it Up – Baby

(Chorus)
Lover Of Mine
Smile If You Lust Me
I'm Right Here Right Now
Ready To Stay In Lust With You
I've Never Had Any Better
So-Lover – I'm-Thinking
Let's Love Shack Together

41

124. The Other

Somebody-Told-Me – That-You
Were-Doing it Again
Out with Somebody-New
All Happy – Hugging on Him
Like He is Your-Man

I'm – Left – Alone
Wondering – Where-You-Were
Trying to Keep – My-Mind
Off the Hurt – You-Give-Me
Every-Time – You-Forget-My – Name

(Chorus)
Woman – Oh woman
Just Call Me The Other
'Cause You Sleep Around So Much
I Know It's So Hard For You
To Remember My Name

I-Say – Forget-You
Don't-Want-You to Come-Back
You've-Done-This – Too-Many-Times
I'm-Tired of the Scars
What's – My – Name

I'm-Such a Fool to Still-Love-You
My-Heart has Been-Hardened
From-All the Pain – You-Give-it
I'm-Tired of the Scars
What's – My – Name

(Chorus)
Woman – Oh woman
Just Call Me The Other
'Cause You Sleep Around So Much
I Know It's So Hard For You
To Remember My Name

No-Way – Am-I – Gonna-Let-You
Rip-My – Heart-Out-Again
You-Might-Think – You'll-Talk-Me
Out of Leaving-You – Today

No – Way – Baby
You're – My – Yesterday
Away – From – You
Is – My – Tomorrow
What's – My – Name
What's – My – Name

(Chorus)
Woman – Oh woman
Just Call Me The Other
'Cause You Sleep Around So Much
I Know It's So Hard For You
To Remember My Name

Somebody-Told-Me – That-You
Were-Doing it Again
Out with Somebody-New
All Happy – Hugging on Him
Like He is Your-Man

I'm – Left – Alone
Wondering – Where-You-Were
Trying to Keep – My-Mind
Off the Hurt – You-Give-Me
Every-Time – You-Forget-My – Name

(Chorus)
Woman – Oh woman
Just Call Me The Other
'Cause You Sleep Around So Much
I Know It's So Hard For You
To Remember My Name

125. Give Her What I Promised

She-Dresses – Hot as Hell
Looking-Like a Goddess
I-Catch – My-Breath
I'm-Ready – She's-Perfect
Have to Go for It

Know for Sure – She's
Heard – Everything – Before
First-Words – I-Give to Her
Has to Be – Just-What
She--Wants to Hear – or
She'll-Make-Me – Crash and Burn

(Chorus)
She's All That
And She Knows It
If I Want To Keep Her
I Got To Be Willing To
Give Her What I Promised

She's-Hot – She's-Cold
Making-Me-Crazy with Desire
She-Lets-Me – Kiss-Her
Only-Enough to Want-More
Get-My-Chance at a Good-Feel
She-Watches – My-Eyes for Greediness

Then-She-Pushes – My-Hands-Away
I-Sit-There – Shaking
Like a Sex-Starved – Man
She-Laughs – I-Got-You
While-She-Waits for Me-To
Properly-Beg – Her-Right

(Chorus)
She's All That
And She Knows It
If I Want To Keep Her
I Got To Be Willing To
Give Her What I Promised

If-I-Want-All – That-She's-Got
I-Have to Be – Willing to Put
My-Balls in a Jar – When-I-Leave
So-She-Knows – I'll-Be – Very-Good

When-She's-Nice – When-She-Lets-Me
Have a Night-Out – With the Boys
When-I-Get-Home – I-Have to Beg
So-Hard – Just to Get-Them – Back

(Chorus)
She's All That
And She Knows It
If I Want To Keep Her
I Got To Be Willing To
Give Her What I Promised
My-Balls In A Jar
Oh-My – Oh-My

She-Dresses – Hot as Hell
Looking-Like a Goddess
I-Catch – My-Breath
I'm-Ready – She's-Perfect
Have to Go for It

Know for Sure – She's
Heard – Everything – Before
First-Words – I-Give to Her
Has to Be – Just-What
She--Wants to Hear – or
She'll-Make-Me – Crash and Burn

(Chorus)
She's All That
And She Knows It
If I Want To Keep Her
I Got To Be Willing To
Give Her What I Promised
My-Balls In A Jar
My-Balls In A Jar
My-Balls In A Jar
Damn What Was I Thinking

45

126. Humping

I-Like – Your-Face
I-Like – Your-Ass
You-Got-It – All-Baby
And-Baby – I-Want the Whole
Package – That is You

With a Blush on Your-Face
You-Tell-Me – You-Need to Wait
I-Kiss-You – I-Tell-You
It's-Ok-Baby
I-Can-Wait – For a Little-While

(Chorus)
The Time Is Now Baby
It's Time To Do Some Humping
We've Waited Long Enough
It's Time To Take Off Our Clothes
Baby Oh Baby – It's Time
For Some Hot-Sweet Humping

Baby – I've-Started a Clock
Inside – My – Mind
Its-Purpose is to Tell-Me
When the Time of Our-Waiting
No-Longer – Applies

Oh-Baby – Wow-Baby
That-Time is Now
I-Feel-It – You're-Ready
By the Way – You're-Looking at Me
Don't-Worry-Baby – I'll-Take it Easy
Believe – Me – Baby
I've-Done-This – Many-Times

(Chorus)
The Time Is Now Baby
It's Time To Do Some Humping
We've Waited Long Enough
It's Time To Take Off Our Clothes
Baby Oh Baby – It's Time
For Some Hot-Sweet Humping

Made-You – Fall in Love with Me
As-I-Whispered – My-Sweet-Talks
You-Fell so Fast it Turned – Me-On
So-I – Gave-You the Night
You-Always – Dreamed of Having

When-We-Were-Through – You-Looked-So
Don't-You-Dare – Leave-Me-Now
I-Stayed – We-Kept-on a Humping
'Til-You-Made-Me – Fall in Love – With-You
Now-We're-Getting-Married
All-Because of Hot-Sweet-Humping

(Chorus)
The Time Is Now Baby
It's Time To Do Some Humping
We've Waited Long Enough
It's Time To Take Off Our Clothes
Baby Oh Baby – It's Time
For Some Hot-Sweet Humping

127. I'm Cursed

Am-I – Really-Going-To
Do-This to Myself – Again
Sometimes – I-Wonder
If-I'm – All-There or Not

I-Know the Truth
I'm-Fine – It's-Them
They-Start-Off so Different
Then in No-Time at All
They are Exactly-Like
What-I've—Just – Ran-Away-From

(Chorus)
I Know I'm Cursed
I Have To be
'Cause Every Time
I Pick Up A New Lady
In A Few Days Time
The Same Awful Woman Reappears

Really the Only-Thing
That is Truly-Different
About-All the Ladies
I've-Known and Dated
Is-What-Lies – Under-Their-Clothes

Some-Fit so Great
It's-Like-Magic
Others – Not so Much
More-Like a Crash
Still-I-Tried – Real-Hard
With a Hard-On
To-Make-Things – Work-Out
But-I – Can't-Help-It

When the Bitch – Reappears
I-Take-Off – Real-Fast
Never-Looking-Back for More
Of the Now – Constantly-Complaining
Not-Good-Enough – In the Sack
For-Me to Take – Anymore – From-The
Same-Woman of My-Nightmares

(Chorus)
I Know I'm Cursed
I Have To be
'Cause Every Time
I Pick Up A New Lady
In A Few Days Time
The Same Awful Woman Reappears

(Chorus)
I Know I'm Cursed
I Have To be
'Cause Every Time
I Pick Up A New Lady
In A Few Days Time
The Same Awful Woman Reappears

128. Love Has Become (A Four Letter Word)

I'm-Not the Best at Love
Most of the Time
During-My-Life
I-Was-Only – Interested
In – Having – Sex

Now that I-Have – Aged
I'm-Looking to Have
Some-Familiar – Stick-Around
But-All – I-Can-Find
Are – Ladies – Wanting
And-Ready to Have-Sex
With-No-Love in Their-Hearts

(Chorus)
I Want To Find Love
Wouldn't You Just Know It
They Only Want Me For Sex
It's Great And Sad That
Love Has Become
A Four Letter Word

It's so Very-True
Life – Repeats – Itself
I was Ready to Leave
When-They – Wanted-Me to Stay

It's a Kick to the Heart
That-My-Life is a Vice-Versa
I-Go-With the Flow
Eagerly-Awaiting the Time
Until-I – Can-Find A Heart
That-I-Can – Seduce with My-Love

(Chorus)
I Want To Find Love
Wouldn't You Just Know It
They Only Want Me For Sex
It's Great And Sad That
Love Has Become
A Four Letter Word

129. Let's Up And Down Together

They-Say – You're-Dirty and Nasty
That-You – Never-Say-No
That-You – Always-Say-Yes
You-Have the Looks
Like-You – Would be so Very
Very-Good for Me

I-Like a Lady that Says-Yes
You're-Very-High on My-List
Of-Greatest-Things on Earth
And-I'm in Need of Greatness
This-Very-Night – All-Night-Long

(Chorus)
Let's Up And Down Together
I Don't Mind At All
That You Never Say No
Let's Up And Down Together
Because Sexy Lady
I'm Never Too Busy To Hear Yes

My-Date is a No-No
I-Want to Hear-Yes-Yes
I-Have – No-Time-Tonight
For-Another-Lady that's Full of No's
So-I-Walk-Over to You

With a Lick of My-Lips
I-Point – My-Finger at My-Pants
Help – You – Understand
That-I'm a Man – That's-Ready
To-Hear a Great-Big-Yes
From a Dirty and Nasty – Lady-Like-You

(Chorus)
Let's Up And Down Together
I Don't Mind At All
That You Never Say No
Let's Up And Down Together
Because Sexy Lady
I'm Never Too Busy To Hear Yes
Call Me Any Time For A Repeat
50

130. So I Broke Your Heart

You-Came-Around – Knocking
Looking for Some-Love
I-Was so Generous – Letting-You-Spend
The-Afternoon – Making-Sweet-Love with Me

Now-You're-Mad at Me
Because-I'm – Done with You
You-Call-Me and Call-Me
Showing-Up – When-I'm – Having-Sex

(Chorus)
So I Broke Your Heart
Stop Complaining About It
Go Find Someone New
To Have Sex With You
So I Broke Your Heart
Stop Complaining About It
Go Find Someone New
To Have Sex With You

Well-Pretty-Baby
Just-Because – You-Have it Fine
Doesn't-Mean – I-Want to Have-You
More-Than-Once – Not-When-There-Are
So-Many-Fine-Ladies – Willing
To-Spend the Afternoon
Having-Hot-Sweet-Sex – With-Me

(Chorus)
So I Broke Your Heart
Stop Complaining About It
Go Find Someone New
To Have Sex With You
So I Broke Your Heart
Stop Complaining About It
Go Find Someone New
To Have Sex With You

Okay-Baby – One-Time
I-Can-Make-Myself-Screw
The-Same-Lady-Twice
Just-Don't-Ask for a Thrice
51

131. The Push That Got Away

I-Said-Hello – Later that Night
Great-Looking from Head to Toe
Said – Yes-You-Can-Touch-Me

What a Night – What a Lady
I-Fell in Lust – After-Our-First-Time
What to Do – What to Do
Can't-Lose this Hot-Honey

Damn – Oh – Damn
Her-Friends – Are-Way-Too – Hot and Horny
For-Me-Not to Screw-Them-Too

(Chorus)
The Push That Got Away
Was the Best Piece I Ever Had
Such A Damn Shame
I Would Love It
If She Would Have Been
The Push That Stayed And Screwed Me

Thirty-Three-Days – Go-By
I've – Been – Half – Good
Only-Screwing-Two of Her-Friends

Third-Friend was Not a Charm
When-Hot-Honey – Found-Us
Screwing-On the Floor

Before-I-Knew-It – I-Was-Out the Door
Begging to Screw-Them-Both
While-Two-Hot-Honeys – Stayed-Friends
'Cause it Was-All – My-Fault

(Chorus)
The Push That Got Away
Was the Best Piece I Ever Had
Such A Damn Shame
I Would Love It
If She Would Have Been
The Push That Stayed And Screwed Me

132. 6 + 1 = 7 Days In A Row

After 6 X's – What-Do-You-Get
Yeah – That's – Right
Looking-Forward to the 7th
Time in a Roll

I-Have-It-So-Good – I-Get-It-So-Fine
Lady-Six-Times – Gave-Me a Call
For a Seventh-Time in a Row
How – Can – I – Say – No

(Chorus)
6 + 1 = 7 Days In A Row
= A Full Week Of Passion
6 + 1 = 7 Days In A Row
= I Never Had To Seek Elsewhere
6 + 1 = 7 Days In A Row
= She Never Said No / She Never Said Stop
Then The Eighth-Day Came
And Just Like That – It All Went Away

Lady-Seven-Times – In-Her-Eyes
I'm – Her – Man – I'm-Her-Reason to Moan
On the Eighth-Day – I-Didn't-Wait for Her-Call
I – Just – Came – A-Knocking at Her-Door

(Me) Open-Up-Baby – I-Want to be Pleased-First
(Her) Go-Away – I've had Enough of You and Your-Lust
(Me) Baby – I-Don't-Understand
(Her) Understand-This – My-Door is Closed to You
(Her) And-So-Are – My-Legs
(Me) How-About-Tomorrow – Baby
(Her) Go-Away

(Chorus)
6 + 1 = 7 Days In A Row
= A Full Week Of Passion
6 + 1 = 7 Days In A Row
= I Never Had To Seek Elsewhere
6 + 1 = 7 Days In A Row
= She Never Said No / She Never Said Stop
Then The Eighth-Day Came
And Just Like That – It All Went Away

133. Don't Worry I Haven't Changed

It's-Been-Awhile-Baby – I-Can-Tell
You're-Shaking from My-Lusting
Sit-Down-Baby – Take-It-Easy
You-Did – Nothing-Wrong
That-Remembered – Flush-You-Feel
Is-Not a Sin – No-Baby – It's a Blessing

Heaven and Hell – Who-Cares
Let-Them – Battle it Out
We're-Only-Doing – What-Our-Bodies
Were-Made to Do – All the Time
So-Let's-Do-It-Again – Before-You-Faint

(Chorus)
That's It Come Back To Me
You Know You Want Me
Don't Worry I Haven't Changed
I Still Got What You Need
To Make You Feel Alive

You've-Changed-Back – Baby
The-Power of My-Lustful-Loving
Is so Powerful – Indeed
Baby – You'll-Care for Nothing but
Having a Lustful – Wonderful-Time

Baby – I'm so Proud of you
With a Dry-Tear in My-Eye
I-Lay-You-Down for What-You-Beg for
You're so Welcome – My-Darling
Remember – You-Love-Me so Much
Even-Though-Baby – I-Don't-Do the Same

(Chorus)
That's It Come Back To Me
You Know You Want Me
Don't Worry I Haven't Changed
I Still Got What You Need
To Make You Feel Alive

54

134. Sparkless

I – Love – You
We've-Been-Together so Long
You-Always-Pick a Time to Be-Sweet
Right-After-You – Bring-Me-Down
From-Hours of Your-Complaining

Now it's Too-Late
No-Way-Can-I – Give-It to You
Even-If – I-Wanted-To
I'm-All-Turned-Off
Mr. Happy has Left the Building

(Chorus)
You Say I'm Sparkless
That I Have No Flame
For You And Our Love
And Right You Are – For You
Don't Turn Me On Anymore
Making Me Sparkless For You

I – Don't – Love – You
Even-Though of All the Years
We-Had – That-Were-Great
Filled with Love and Fun
They-Were so Long-Ago
That-I-Hardly – Remember-Them

I-Try-My-Best – I-Really-Did
But-Now-Baby
I-Don't-Care-Anymore
Because of the Misery of
Living-With-Your-Hell

(Chorus)
You Say I'm Sparkless / That I Have No Flame
For You And Our Love / And Right You Are – For You
Don't Turn Me On Anymore / Making Me Sparkless For You

(Spoken)
Love that Turns to Sparkless / Is Like a Large-Empty-Void
That-You-Might-Never / Fill to Full-Again – Making
All-You-Can-Do is Shake / Your-Head to the Sadness of it All

135. Roar Out Your Hell

Life-Sucks – It-Always-Will
Don't-Let-That – Bring-You-Down
There's-Always-Time
To-Go-Out and Get-Laid
Instead of Sulking at Home

All-Alone – Sitting-There
In-Front of a Screen
Watching-What – Other-People
Put-Up for You to See
As-They – Live-Their-Lives
Never-Thinking – About-You

(Chorus)
Pick It Up You're Dragging
You're Not That Damn Old
Dust Your Tired Ass Off
Grab Your Balls – Beat Your Chest
As You Fully – Roar Out Your Hell
Come On Man – Roar Out Your Hell
Or Are You Just Waiting – For Death
To Come Around And Take Your Life

Screen-Watching is Fun – It's-Ok for Awhile
Looking at a Real-Person – Not Just the Image of Them
Well – You-Get – All-Kinds of Perks – Like-Their-Sweet-Scent
Like-Their-Soft-Touch – That-Turns-You-On

If You're-Lucky – If-She Feels-Sorry for You
Well – You-Just-Might-Reach-Out
And-Grab-Yourself a Nice-Slice
Of the Promise-Land

(Chorus)
Pick It Up You're Dragging
You're Not That Damn Old
Dust Your Tired Ass Off
Grab Your Balls – Beat Your Chest
As You Fully – Roar Out Your Hell
Come On Man – Roar Out Your Hell
Or Are You Just Waiting – For Death
To Come Around And Take Your Life

I Remember Rock And Roll (906.) (Extra Bonus)

Memories of Long-Ago in My-Mind
Calling-Me-Back-Through-Time
To-Forget-All-My-Heavies
To-Party-Hardy and Rock-On
Like-My-Life is On the Line

I-Remember – Oh-Yes-I-Do
Summer-Time – Back-Seat-Loving
I-Remember – Oh-Yes-I-Do
Summer-Time – Skinny-Dipping
I-Remember – Oh-Yes-I-Do
Summer-Time – Falling in Lust
And-I-Remember – And-I-Remember
Rock – And – Roll

(Chorus)
I Remember Rock And Roll
And What It Did For My Soul
I Remember Rock And Roll
It Kept Me Young And Free
I Remember Rock And Roll
Like A Yesterday's Dream Come True
I Remember Rock And Roll
So I'm Going To Start
Rock And Rolling Again
'Til The Day I Die

Memories of Long-Ago in My-Mind
Calling-Me-Back-Through-Time
To-Forget-All-My-Heavies
To-Party-Hardy and Rock-On
Like-My-Life is On the Line

I-Remember – Oh-Yes-I-Do
Summer-Time – Back-Seat-Loving
I-Remember – Oh-Yes-I-Do
Summer-Time – Skinny-Dipping
I-Remember – Oh-Yes-I-Do
Summer-Time – Falling in Lust
And-I-Remember – And-I-Remember
Rock – And – Roll
(Repeat Chorus)

136. Rocking & Rolling

Wow – What a Lady
Can't-Keep – My-Eyes-Off-Her
She-Looks so Lovely
She has Such a Pretty-Face
With a Body – Built for Thrills

I'm so Drawn to Her
Have to Take – My-Shot
Can't-Let the Chance – of
Perfect-Love-Making
Slip-Away – From-My-Pants

(Chorus)
Rocking And Rolling
Moaning And Groaning
Come On Baby Let's Go For It
I Want To Have So much Fun
Making Love To You
All Night Long – 'Til Forever

She is So-Perfect – She is So-Sweet
With--Such a Lovely-Voice – Talking to Me
Watching as Her-Cheeks-Blush
From-Knowing – What-I-Want from Her

(Chorus)
Rocking And Rolling
Moaning And Groaning
Come On Baby Let's Go For It
I Want To Have So much Fun
Making Love To You
All Night Long – 'Til Forever

My-Place – Your-Place
Come on Baby – That's-It
No-Better-Time – Than-This
Just-Keep-Looking at Me
I-Will-Make-You-Float
I-Know – I-Got-What-You-Need
To-Make-You-Explode

(Repeat Chorus)

Rocking & Rolling (Second Rocking Version)

Wow-Who's-That – Wow-What a Lady
Butterfly – Tattoo on Her-Ankle
Green-Eyes and Raven-Hair
Look at That-Body – She-Even
Has an Extra-Long – Tongue

Don't-Know-Her – But-I've-Been
Waiting for Her – My-Whole-Life
Rock & Roll – Think-I'll Sing-Her
My – Rocking & Rolling – Song
Hey – Baby

(Chorus)
Rocking & Rolling
Moaning & Groaning
Come On Baby Let's Go For It
I Want To Have So Much Fun
Rocking & Rolling – With-You

Crystal-Green-Eyes – Turns to Blood-Red
A-Whisper then a Hiss
I – Can-Not – Move
She's-Hot – She's-Evil – She's-Hot
I-Think-I-Love-Her

Bite-Me – Taste-My-Blood
But-Baby – Sweet-Evil-Lady
Let's-Screw – After-That
Before-You-Decide to Kill-Me

Hey – Baby – Let-Me-Sing-You-My
Rocking & Rolling – Song
Maybe it Will-Make a Difference

(Chorus)
Rocking & Rolling
Moaning & Groaning
Come On Baby Let's Go For It
I Want To Have So Much Fun
Rocking & Rolling – With-You

137. Dancing Sexsation

Nobody-Sees-You
Nobody-Knows-You
Dancing-Sexsation
Nobody-Loves-You
The-Way-I-Love-You

Dance – Dance – Dance
Take – Off – Your – Clothes
You're-My-Dream-Come-True
Dancing-Sexsation – I-Love-You

(Chorus)
Dancing Sexsation
You're Such A Star / Dancing On Stage
Wearing Just Your Sexy Flesh
Dancing Sexsation
You're Such A Star / Dancing On Stage
Just For Me And My Love

Dancing-Sexsation – It's-10:15
Time for My – Lap-Dance
Ride-Me – Entice-Me
Dancing Sexsation
I-Know-You-Want-Me
Not-Just-My – Green-Dollars

(Chorus)
Dancing Sexsation
You're Such A Star / Dancing On Stage
Wearing Just Your Sexy Flesh
Dancing Sexsation
You're Such A Star / Dancing On Stage
Just For Me And My Love

Oh-No –Dancing-Sexsation
Tell-Me it Ain't-So
Where-Did-That
Wedding-Ring – Come-From
Dancing Sexsation
You are No-Longer – My-Star

(Repeat Chorus)
60

Dancing Sexsation (First Dance Remix)

Fire in My-Heart
Bulge in My-Pants
You-Look so Sexy and Built
On-Stage-Naked and All-Alone
Reaching-Out for My – Green-Dollars

Dance – Dance – Dance
Your-Life is a Living-Sin
As-You – Live it Free
You're the Perfect-Woman

(Chorus)
Dancing Sexsation
You're Such A Star / Dancing On Stage
Wearing Just Your Sexy Flesh
Dancing Sexsation
You're Such A Star / Dancing On Stage
Just For Me And My Love

Ask-You-Out – Every-Night
Why-I-Do-Not-Know
You-Always-Say-No
Fire and Ice / You-Give-Me-Everything
Leaving-Me-With-Nothing – But-My-Lonely-Desire

(Chorus)
Dancing Sexsation
You're Such A Star / Dancing On Stage
Wearing Just Your Sexy Flesh
Dancing Sexsation
You're Such A Star / Dancing On Stage
Just For Me And My Love

Oh-No –Dancing-Sexsation
Your-Loser-Husband is Back
Tell-Me it Ain't-So
So-Sad – The-Love of My-Life
Is-Just-Another – Fool in Love
Goodbye-Dancing-Sexsation
You are No-Longer – My-Star

(Repeat Chorus)
61

138. Love Is Too Slow (To Ever Catch Me)

Ladies and More-Ladies
Been-Trying for Years
To-Get – Their-Claws in Me
I've-Let-Them – Get-Close
Sometimes too Damn-Close
Just so I – Could-Get
What-I – Always-Want

Ladies and More-Ladies
Seem to Never-Learn
I'm-Not-Interested in Love
Just-What's – In their Panties
A-Pretty-Face – Makes-Me-Stop
A-Hot-Naked – Sexy-Body
Makes-Me – Stick-Around

(Chorus)
No Way – No How
I'm Way Too Fast For It
Even Though It's On My Tail
Love Is A Bitch – And
Love Is Too Slow
To Ever Catch Me

Ladies and More-Ladies
Have-Gotten – Mad as Hell
For-Having – Sex-With-Them
Then-Taking the Hell-Off – Real-Fast

So-Upset – With-Tears in Their-Eyes
Telling-All – Their-Friends
Of the Fast-Damn – Bastard
That-Used-Them and Broke-Their-Hearts

(Chorus)
No Way – No How
I'm Way Too Fast For It
Even Though It's On My Tail
Love Is A Bitch – And
Love Is Too Slow
To Ever Catch Me

Ladies and More-Ladies
Have-Tried to Bring-Me-Down
With – Their – Tears
Thinking-I'll – Turn-Soft

Allowing-Them – Their-Chance
To-Be the One and Only
To the Best-Screw – They-Ever-Had

Well-Ladies – You-Know-What
I-Always – Say to That

(Chorus)
No Way – No How
I'm Way Too Fast For It
Even Though It's On My Tail
Love Is A Bitch – And
Love Is Too Slow
To Ever Catch Me

(Bleeds Into Rock and Roll Bachelor)

Hello-Ladies – I'm-Here –Your
Rock and Roll Bachelor
Ready to Have a Great-Time
With a Bunch of Fine-Ladies
That-Have – No-Problem
Waiting for Their-Turn

So-Lick-Your-Lips
While-Shaking – Your-Hips
The-Lady with the Best-Ass
Gets to Be – Pleased-First

(Chorus)
Work Hard – Party Harder
Sleep A Little Bit
Eat When I Have The Time
I'm The Ready For Anything
And Can Go Anytime
Rock And Roll Bachelor
Come Rock And Roll With Me

139. The Death Of My Package

I-Tell-You-This
Pain is a Great-Motivator
Everything was Going so Great
I was Doing-Nothing
But-Getting-It-On – All the Time

Then – One – Day
What-I've – Been-Doing
Got-Around the Streets
Turning-All – My-Ladies
Against-Me and My-Package

(Chorus)
Life Can Be Hell
When Ten Ladies
I Loved And Used
Come Screaming And Demanding
For – The Death Of My Package

Ladies-I've-Learned – My-Lesson
Ladies-Please – No-More
This is So – Unlike-You
Untie-Me and Put
All-Those – Weapons-Away

Ladies-I've-Learned – My-Lesson
Ladies-Please – No-More
Think-About – What-You're-Doing
Ladies if You – Cut it Off – All-Nasty
None of You – Will-Ever
Be-Able to Enjoy-It – Again

(Chorus)
Life Can Be Hell
When Ten Ladies
I Loved And Used
Come Screaming And Demanding
For – The Death Of My Package

Untied and Free – I-Run-Like-Hell
With-My-Hand on My-Package
Hell-With-It – I-Don't-Care
They-Can-Have – My-Apartment
They-Can-Have – All-My-Shit

I-Have-All – I-Truly-Need
Running-Along-With-Me
I'll-Keep on Running
'Til-I-Get – As-Far-Away as Possible
From-Any-Lady – That-Wants
The-Death of My-Package

(Chorus)
Life Can Be Hell
When Ten Ladies
I Loved And Used
Come Screaming And Demanding
For – The Death Of My Package

(Bleeds Into Rock and Roll Bachelor)

Being the Longest-Best
Is-Easy – On-My – Happy-Soul
Knowing – That-I-Provide
Such-Good – Good – Lovin'
To so Many-Fine – Fine – Ladies
Almost-Brings – Tears to My-Eyes

But-I'm the Rock and Roll – Bachelor
Only-Tears that I-Ever-See
Are-From the Sweet-Ladies – That-Make-Them
After-I've – Pleased-Them – Passionately
Leaving-Them-Alone for the Next-One in Line

(Chorus)
Work Hard – Party Harder
Sleep A Little Bit
Eat When I Have The Time
I'm The Ready For Anything
And Can Go Anytime
Rock And Roll Bachelor
Come Rock And Roll With Me

65

140. Blind Date #1

(Me)
Lonely-Man – Lonely-Heart
Looking for Passion – That's-Who-I-Am
I'm-Taking a Big-Chance – Tonight
Taking a Number – From a Friend

Blind-Date – What-Do-I-Have to Lose
Hope-She's-Hot – Hope-She-Puts-Out
Hope-She's-Not-Crazy or a Tease

(Chorus)
No More – Never Again
What A Crazy Blind Date
This Crazy Lady Turned Out To Be
She Gave My Car Away
She Even Made Me
Get My Ass Kicked

(Blind Date)
Be-Quiet – While-Tied-Up
Here-Let-Me – Paint-Your-Face
That's-Better – You-Look so Pretty

What's-Your-Problem – You-Have a Blind-Date
Not-Any-More – I'm-Taking-Your-Place
Lucky-Man – He's-Going to Have
The-Night of His-Life

(Chorus)
No More – Never Again
What A Crazy Blind Date
This Crazy Lady Turned Out To Be
She Gave My Car Away
She Even Made Me
Get My Ass Kicked

(Police Dispatch)
Be on the Look-Out – For a Woman – In-Her-Late-Twenties
She is Wanted for Breaking and Entering
She is Wanted for Assault / She-Ties-Up-Her-Victims
Leaves-Them in the Bathroom / While-She-Takes-Over
Their-Lives for a Few-Days and Up to a Week

(Me) Hello-I'm
(Blind-Date) I-Don't-Care – Come on In
(Me) You-Look-Great – I-Like-Your-Dress
(Blind-Date) Not-Me – It's-Ugly – I'm-Changing
Sit-Down – Help-Me-Pick-Out the Perfect-Dress
Are-You-Thirsty – Follow-Me – Drink-From-My-Sink
(Me) No-Thanks – I'm-Not-That-Thirsty
(Blind-Date) I'm-Hungry – Let's-Go-Eat

(Chorus)
No More – Never Again
What A Crazy Blind Date
This Crazy Lady Turned Out To Be
She Gave My Car Away
She Even Made Me
Get My Ass Kicked

(Me) Here's-My-Car – What-Are-You-Doing
(Blind-Date) I'm-Runnning – Watch-Me-Run
(Me) You're-Back – That-Was-Great
(Blind-Date) I'm so Fast – No-One-Can-Catch-Me
(Me) Where-Are-You-Going-Now
(Blind-Date) I'm-Runnning – Watch-Me-Run
(Me) You're-Back – Are-You-Though-Running
Do-You-Want-Some – Din-Din
(Blind-Date) Yes-I-Want-My – Din-Din

(Chorus)
No More – Never Again
What A Crazy Blind Date
This Crazy Lady Turned Out To Be
She Gave My Car Away
She Even Made Me
Get My Ass Kicked

(Me) Do-You-Like-Your-Dinner
(Blind-Date) Your-Chicken is Staring at My-Chicken
Make it Stop – Make it Stop – Make it Stop
(Me) My-Chicken-Dinner – Doesn't-Have-Eyes
(Blind-Date) Too-Late – Now-They-Have to Fight
(Me) What – No-Don't-Throw – My-Chicken on the Floor
(Blind-Date) My-Chicken-Won – Your-Chicken is a Loser
(Me) Why-Me – I-Have a Headache – Damn-My-Balls-Itch
(Blind-Date) Well-Pull-Them-Out and Scratch-Them – I'll-Watch

(Chorus)
No More – Never Again
What A Crazy Blind Date
This Crazy Lady Turned Out To Be
She Gave My Car Away
She Even Made Me
Get My Ass Kicked

(Me)
Took a Piss – Came-Back – My-Date was Gone
Crazy-Lady – Stole-My-Car – I-Hate-Her
Nothing-I-Can-Do-But-Walk – Hope-I-Find-Her
Here-She-Comes-Walking-Towards-Me
Where-The-Hell is My-Car

(Blind-Date) Hello – Do-I-Know-You
(Me) Yes-You-Do – I'm-Your-Blind-Date
(Blind-Date) I-Thought-You-Looked-Familiar
(Me) Well-Crazy-Lady – Where the **** is My-Car
(Blind-Date) I-Gave it Away – They-Had-No-Car
(Me) What – Who – Where the**** are They-At
(Blind-Date) Over-There – Don't-They-Look so Nice

(Chorus)
No More – Never Again
What A Crazy Blind Date
This Crazy Lady Turned Out To Be
She Gave My Car Away
She Even Made Me
Get My Ass Kicked

(Me) Hey-Guys – This is My-Car
(Guys) Not-Any-More – Get the **** Out of Here
(Me) Glad-To – But-Not-Without-My-Car
(Guys) Leave ****** or It's-Your-Ass
(Me) ****-You
(Guys) You-Bleed-Real-Good – ****-It
Here's-Your-Keys and a Beer
(Me) Thanks-Guys – I-Could-Use-It

(Chorus)
No More – Never Again / What A Crazy Blind Date
This Crazy Lady Turned Out To Be / She Gave My Car Away
She Even Made Me / Get My Ass Kicked

(Blind-Date) Are-You-Done – I'm-Bored – Take-Me-Home
(Me) Suck-My – Never-Mind – You'll-Probably-Eat-It – Let's-Go
(Blind-Date) I'm-Not-Hungry-Stupid – I'm-Bored-With-You
(Me) Well-Crazy-Din-Din-Lady – Why-Didn't-You-Say-So
It-Would-Just-Break-My-Heart – If-You-Were-Bored
(Blind-Date) That's so Sweet – I-Guess-You-Can – ****-Me
Well-Just-Don't-Stand-There – Times-A-Wasting
(Me) Follow-You – Later-Guys – Freaking-Blind-Dates

(Chorus)
No More – Never Again
What A Crazy Blind Date
This Crazy Lady Turned Out To Be
She Gave My Car Away
She Even Made Me
Get My Ass Kicked

(Blind-Date) Home-Sweet-Home – Before-We-Go-Inside
I-Have to Warn-You – Try-Not to Blink – While-Having-Sex-With-Me
(Me) I'll-Do-My-Best – I'm-Just-Wondering – Do-You-Have
All-Your-Body-Parts – Do-You-Glow in The-Dark
(Blind-Date) Yes-I-Do – And-Not-Anymore – I've-Been-Cured
(Me) Okay-Then-Let's-Go – Before-You-Turn-Into a Pumpkin

(Chorus)
No More – Never Again
What A Crazy Blind Date
This Crazy Lady Turned Out To Be
She Gave My Car Away
She Even Made Me
Get My Ass Kicked

(The Police)
Stay-Right-Where-You-Are – You're-Under-Arrest
Grab-Ahold of Her – She's-Getting-Away

(Blind-Date) I'm-Runnning – Watch-Me-Run
I'm so Fast – No-One-Can-Catch-Me – ****-You-Pigs
(Me) Good-Bye – Crazy-Din-Din-Lady – Hope-You-Get-Away

(Chorus)
No More – Never Again / What A Crazy Blind Date
This Crazy Lady Turned Out To Be / She Gave My Car Away
She Even Made Me / Get My Ass Kicked

Horny Animal Man (13.)

Baby-You-Look so Fine
Sitting-Here-Together
I-Know – You-Can-Feel-It
Let's-Get-Undressed
I-Want – What-You-Got
Show-It-To-Me – Show-It-To-Me

Oh-Yeah – Let-Me-Tell-You
Pretty-Lady – You-Are so Lucky
You-Have – The-Face and The-Ass
Twice the Nice – For-Me to Enjoy

(Chorus)
Baby – I'm A Horny Animal Man
Baby – I Like To Sex It Up
Baby – I'm A Horny Animal Man
Baby – I Like To Sex It Up
Baby – I'm A Horny Animal Man
First – We'll Get It On – Then-I'll-Get-Gone

Sexy-Lady – I'm-Finished – With-You
Sexy-Lady – I-Have to Stand – Back-Up-Now
Sexy-Lady – You-Were-So-Great
Sexy-Lady – I-Have to Put – My-Clothes-Back-On
Sexy-Lady – I-Need to Take-Off
Goodbye to You – Sexy-Lady

No-Need to Worry-Baby – You-Look-Even-Better
Than-You-Did – Before-We-Had-Our-Great-Time

(Chorus)
Baby – I'm A Horny Animal Man
Baby – I Like To Sex It Up
Baby – I'm A Horny Animal Man
Baby – I Like To Sex It Up
Baby – I'm A Horny Animal Man
First – We'll Get It On – Then-I'll-Get-Gone

Baby – I'm a Horny-Animal-Man – I'll-Never-Be a Another-Way
Baby – I'm a Horny-Animal-Man – Maybe-I'll-Return – Someday

(Bonus Song)
Too Damn Ugly To Get One (298.)

All-I-Hear – From a Pretty-Lady-Is
You're a Really-Nice-Guy – But
I-See-You – More as a Friend

Besides – We-Wouldn't – Want to Ruin
Our – Great – Friendship
By-Doing-Something – That-Neither of Us
Really – Wants to Happen

I-Tell-Her – I-Understand – Smiling
As-I-Receive – My-Just-Friends-Hug
Wishing-Once – She'd-Say – Yes – Why-Not

(Chorus)
Why Does It Seem
That The Only Ones – I Can Get
Are The Ones – I Don't Want
I Want A Pretty Lady – But I'm
Too Damn Ugly To Get One

Yeah-I'm-Ugly – I-Know-This
And so Does-Your-Women
But-That-Don't-Stop-Me
From-Snagging-Them-Up

When-You-Leave-Them
Use and Cheat on Them
I-Just-Keep – Buying-Them-Drinks
'Til-I-Start – Looking-Good to Their-Red-Eyes

Then-I-Take-Them-Home
Introduce-Them – To-My-Bed of Pleasure
Where-I'm-Great – Until-First-Morning-Light

(Chorus)
Why Does It Seem
That The Only Ones – I Can Get
Are The Ones – I Don't Want
I Want A Pretty Lady – But I'm
Too Damn Ugly To Get One

71

Discography (Pages 72-76)

Books 1 Through 7 Song Listing
Book One: **Who Am I?** – 1-20
Book Two: **Mind Rockin'** – 21-40
Book Three: **Big Time Love** – 41-60
Book Four: **Love High** – 61-80
Book Five: **Siphon Your Minds** – 81-100
Book Six: **Do You Remember Rock And Roll?** – 101-120
Book Seven: **Rock And Roll Bachelor** – 121-140
(Example) **01.** = Original Numbering – **07.** = Book Numbering

01. I Must Go Away - 07. - Book 1
02. A Race Called Man - 03. - Book 1
03. Across The Sky (Edited Version) - 17. - Book 1
05. Justice (Edited Version) - 34. - Book 2
07. Bleeding My Beast Blood Upon the Floor - **20.** - Book 1
08. I Am Wolf - 18. - Book 1
13. Horny Animal Man **(Bonus S. No Book #)** - Book 7
23. Empty Hands (Edited Version) - 36. - Book 2
26. Me Myself & I - 13. - Book 1
33. Enjoy (The Eye) - 90. - Book 5
38. Darken Our Love (Edited Version) - 27. - Book 2
40. Our Love - 45. - Book 3
41. All I Need - 06. - Book 1
43. Love, Baby Love - 63 - Book 4
45. Cursed Years - 04. - Book 1
47. I'm Dying And It's Raining - 14. - Book 1
49. Rip You Apart While Drinking You Down - 19. - Book 1

54. Speak As One - 16. - Book 1
55. Push Me Away - 44. - Book 3
59. We The People - 15. - Book 1
61. Bam Burn Dead Hell (Edited Version) - 38. - Book 2
64. We Are Here - 31. - Book 2
65. The Church of No God (Edited Version) - 32. - Book 2
66. Sweet Sweet Love - 68. - Book 4
67. Who Am I? - 01. - Book 1
70. Shout (Your Day Will Come) - 02. - Book 1
72. Thickness of Mind - 22. - Book 2
73. Rock And Roll House - 10. - Book 1
74. Hero - 12. - Book 1
75. I'll Be Your Hero - 11. - Book 1
76. Tapped (Edited Version) - 30. - Book 2
77. Why - 05. - Book 1

78. Love Den (Not A Sin) (Single Version) - 08. - Book 1
79. Angel Eyes (Single Version) - 09. - Book 1
80. I Am Dream / Prelude To The Eye - 91. - Book 5
81. Stranger Calling No One - 23. - Book 2
83. Set Loose on Hell (S.L.O.H. #1) - **40.** - Book 2
84. Freaking Zombies Man - 39. - Book 2
86. Through the Flame of a Candle - 29. - Book 2
87. I love You - 26. - Book 2
96. Break Me When You're Done - 28. - Book 2
97. She Let Me Pick Her - 72. - Book 4
98. The Last Rocker - 24. - Book 2

100. Purgatory (20 Steps) (The Single) **(Purgatory's Full: No Book #)**
105. Dying While Texting - 25. - Book 2
111. 3 Can Corn Man - 35. - Book 2
113. Evil Pill - 37. - Book 2
118. Do You Remember Rock And Roll - 111. - Book 6
122. Mind Rockin' - 21. - Book 2
126. Pets and Monsters - 33. - Book 2
127. You Are My Everything - 46. - Book 3
129. Cave Man - 113. - Book 6
132. She's Got To Be Mine   - 62. - Book 4
142. Beautiful - 54. - Book 3
144. Rock Is Good (Take One) **(Bonus S. No Book #)** - Book 6
146. Bounty Hunter - 119. - Book 6
156. I Can Smell Your Death - 94. - Book 5
157. I Can Sense Your Death - 95. - Book 5
166. Brave Face - 93. - Book 5
168. The Push That Got Away - 131. - Book 7
171. It Don't Matter - 103. - Book 6
173. Rock Seem Dead - 102. - Book 6
181. Stain - 104. - Book 6
182. Protector - 86. - Book 5
183. Blind Date #1 - **140.** - Book 7
185. Earth Prisoner (# Way Too Many) - **120.** - Book 6
196. Return To Hell - 114. - Book 6
199. Love - 52. - Book 3

205. Rocking & Rolling - 136. - Book 7
206. Freedom's Mountain - 110. - Book 6
207. Pillow Talk - 69. - Book 4
208. Birth - 96. - Book 5
209. Life - 97. - Book 5
210. Death - 98. - Book 5

214. Coming Home - 105. - Book 6
216. The Other - 124. - Book 7
217. Catch My Heart - 48. - Book 3
224. I Write The Lyrics (Who Cares) - 117. - Book 6
238. Time - 64. - Book 4
239. Stay - 65. - Book 4
240. Dressed Up Like A Diner - 83. - Book 5
249. Long Love Train Ride - 84. - Book 5
250. One Day (The Hard/We Can Do It/Our Time Is Here) - 57. - Book 3
252. Roar Out Your Hell - 135. - Book 7
253. The Lovers Of Forever - **60.** - Book 3
257. Love Is Too Slow For Me - 138. - Book 7
260. Peace Freaks (Gift #4 No Book #) - Book 1
261. Ordinary - 50. - Book 3
266. The Big Bang **(Bonus S. No Book #)** - Book 5
287. Power To The Mammals Who Don't Walk On Two Legs - 85. - Book 5
298. Too Damn Ugly To Get One **(Bonus S. No Book #)** - Book 7

300. Siphon - 81. - Book 5
313. Coma Made For Me - 82. - Book 5
314. Rock And Roll Bachelor - 121. - Book 7
315. One More Time - 122. - Book 7
319. Let's Be Friends (That Sleep Together) - 76. - Book 4
320. Forget About Our Love - 77. - Book 4
323. Little By Little (Duet) - 43. - Book 3
327. High With Me - 66. - Book 4
328. Two Crazy Lovers - 108. - Book 6
341. Fall In Love With Me - 56. - Book 3
344. Flush It (Stupid Stool Samples) - 118. - Book 6
346. Lady From Space (Love Version) - **80.** - Book 4
353. Give Her What I Promised - 125. - Book 7
361. It's So Nice To Be Loved - 42. - Book 3
381. Somebody Loves Me - 47. - Book 3
382. Big Time Love - 41. - Book 3
386. Love Has Become A Four Letter Word - 128. - Book 7
394. Wrap My Love All Around You - 58. - Book 3

405. The Death Of My Package - 139. - Book 7
410. Humping - 126. - Book 7
411. I'm Cursed - 127. - Book 7
413. Still Caught In A Dream **(Bonus S. No Book #)** - Book 5
420. A Beautiful Woman - 55. - Book 3
421. Afraid Of Love - 51. - Book 3
422. Happy Birthday Baby - 71. - Book 4

451. It's Time For Love - 75. - Book 4
456.0 Charity Is More Than A Word (Gift #3 No Book #) - Book 1
457. (I'm Busted) For I've Fallen In Love With You - 67. - Book 4
459. Sparkless - 134. - Book 7
467. Let's Love Shack Together - 123. - Book 7
476. 6 + 1 = 7 Days In A Row - 132 - Book 7
489. Take My Hand - 49. - Book 3
493. I Want To Be With You **(Bonus S. No Book #)** - Books 3 & 4
496. The Entity Of Light - 87. - Book 5
497. Lovely Heaven And Hated Hell - 88. - Book 5
498. The Entity Of Darkness - 89. - Book 5
499. Earth Like Planets Everywhere - 90. - Book 5

502. Makes Me Smile - 74. - Book 4
506. One Life, Rock On - 107. - Book 6
507. Wrecking Ball - 109. - Book 6
508. The Time Is Now **(Bonus S. No Book #)** - Books 3 & 4
519. Don't Worry I Haven't Changed - 133. - Book 7
522. Turn Me On Baby - 78. - Book 4
524. Dancing Sexsation - 137. - Book 7
528. Your Canvas Is Your Soul - 115. - Book 6
529. Let's Up And Down Together - 129. - Book 7
533. When Death Rules the World (Gift #1 No Book #) - Book 2
536. Love High - 61. - Book 4
540. Summer Time And Love - 70. - Book 4
558. She Still Has That Body - 79. - Book 4
561. Love Comes Back Around - 59. - Book 3
563. If You Need Me - 53. - Book 3
566. So I Broke Your Heart - 130. - Book 7
567. Peace and Death (Gift #2 No Book #) - Book 2
576. I Am The Rock (That Likes To Roll) - 106. - Book 6
578. Smile If You Love Me - 73. - Book 4
579. Rocking The World - 101. - Book 6
580. Rock And Roll House #2 (507 Songs Later) - 116. - Book 6
581. Rock Is Good (Take Two) - 112. - Book 6
583. Crash Landed On Their Planet - 99. - Book 5
584. Humans In Space - **100.** - Book 5
586. The Last Rocker #2 **(New S. No Book #)** - Between Books 6 & 7
587. Rock Is Good (Take Three) **(Bonus S. No Book #)** - Book 6
588. The Last Rocker #3 **(New S. No Book #)** - Between Book 6 & 7

856. Failure To Rock **(Bonus S. No Book #)** - Books 6 & 7
(Never Have Sex With A Demon Trilogy:) (863-865)
863. Demon Slayer **(Bonus S. No Book #)** - Book 5
864. Demon Lover **(Bonus S. No Book #)** - Book 5
865. Give Me Another Chance God / I'm A Demon Now
    (Bonus S. No Book #) - Book 5
877. Sex Warrior **(Bonus S. No Book #)** - Books 6 & 7
889. Buy Me A Beer (You Bastard) **(Bonus S. No Book #)** - Books 6 & 7

906. I Remember Rock And Roll **(Bonus S. No Book #)** - Book 1
908. Rock My Bone **(Bonus S. No Book #)** - Books 6 & 7

Quotes (From Original Cover Editions)

Book One: Who Am I? & Book Two: Mind Rockin'
Quote #1
Let's Shout It Out And Speak As One.
Mind Rock On, The Gemini One.

Book Three: Big Time Love & Book Four: Love High
Quote #2
Catch My Heart And Take My Hand
To Find Yourself Some Big Time Love.

Purgatory's Full
Quote #3
Open Up Your Mind Rockin' Minds To The Cold Hard
Reality That Is My Songs & Dreams.

Book Six: Do You Remember Rock And Roll &
Book Seven: Rock And Roll Bachelor
Quote #4
For A Mind Rockin' Good Time, Enjoy Some
Rockin' With The Rock And Roll Bachelor.

Book Five: Siphon Your Minds &
The Vegetarian And The Slaughterhouse

Quote #5
Come On In And Let The Gemini One
Siphon Your Mind Rockin' Minds.

Sex Warrior (877.) (New Cover Bonus)

Been-There – Done-That
That's-Who-I-Am
I-Don't-Even-Have-To
Take-Off-My-Pants
To-Get-It – Real-Quick

Don't-Believe-Me – Well-Then
Let's-Have-A-Sexual-War
Right-Here-On-The-Floor
Begging-Will-Only-Make-Me
Make-You – Moan-Even-Louder

(Chorus)
I'm A Sex Warrior – Baby
That Has Just Sexually Conquered You
Good Luck With Walking The Same
Can You Even Remember Your Name
Better Hurry And Retreat – Baby
'Cause I'm A Sex Warrior
That Never Fires A Pre-Warning Shot

Just-Un-Zip – I'm-Ready-To-Go
I-Get-So-Much – Fine-Tail
I've-Ran-Out-Of-Room
I-Have-To-Come-Over-To-Your-House
Mark-My-Victory – On-Your-Bed-Post

Don't-Believe-Me – Well-Then
Let's-Have-A-Sexual-War
Right-Here-On-The-Floor
Begging – Will-Only-Make-Me
Make-You – Moan-Even-Louder

(Chorus)
I'm A Sex Warrior – Baby
That Has Just Sexually Conquered You
Good Luck With Walking The Same
Can You Even Remember Your Name
Better Hurry And Retreat – Baby
'Cause I'm A Sex Warrior
That Never Fires A Pre-Warning Shot

Buy Me A Beer (You Bastard) (889.) (New Cover Bonus)

Hey-How-You-Doing
That's-Good – That's-Good
No-You-Don't-Know-Me
I'm-Broke and Thirsty
Buy-Me a Beer – I'm-Thirsty-Enough
To-Even Drink – With-You

(Pre-Chorus)
Down On My Luck / Crashed My Truck
Old Lady Left Me / My Pockets Are Empty
I-Need – A-Freaking-Beer

(Chorus)
Buy Me A Beer
Buy Me A Beer You Bastard
Buy Me A Whiskey
Buy Me A Whiskey You Bastard
Buy Me Another Beer
Before I Puke And Pass Out

Have to Tell-You – You're-All-Right
Long as the Whiskey's-Pouring
I-Have-No-Worries – 'Cause-I'm-Drunk
But-One-Thing – Is-On-My-Mind
If-You-Want-Me – To-Do – Your-Old-Lady
You'll-Have to Buy-Me – A-Bottle for Afterwards

(Pre-Chorus)
Down On My Luck / Crashed My Truck
Old Lady Left Me / My Pockets Are Empty
I-Need – A-Freaking-Beer

(Chorus)
Buy Me A Beer
Buy Me A Beer You Bastard
Buy Me A Whiskey
Buy Me A Whiskey You Bastard
Buy Me Another Beer
Before I Puke And Pass Out

Down On My Luck / Crashed My Truck /Buy Me A Beer You Bastard
Old Lady Left Me / Buy Me A Beer / Buy Me A Beer You Bastard

Do You Remember Rock And Roll (Story Version)

Such a great time I had back in the eighties. I was the kinda guy that liked to rock and roll, getting as much tail as I could. Partying all the time, just having a great time, until the next phase of my life. Which never came because I hard rocked myself to my death. Keeping my party going all the way up to Heaven, I arrived. God shook his head, he then walked up to me and smacked me across my head. God grabbed ahold of me and walked me over to the edge of Heaven. He pushed my head down south, so I could check Hell out. God smacked me across the head one more time, then we drank a beer and smoked a bowl of some fine Heavenly funk. Then lastly, I received my job.

I come back to Earth your winged rock Angel, rolling my spirituality down upon your life. I'm so sad to see that you're dragging yourself day in and day out, doing nothing but the same. Don't feel bad. While up in heaven I would look down at all my living rockin' brothers and sisters, same dullness everywhere, rock and roll nowhere to be found.

I'm not saying you have to be like me, just doing nothing but partying and rocking and rolling. No not at all, I'm saying to you, bring it back into your life. Let the beats and the words, wake you up inside. Have a little back of what you used to have inside you. Mortal, Earth brother just grab rock and roll up, store it up nice and safe, using its rockin' purity to enhance your life. Soon the power of rock and roll will soften your soul, making you believe in its pure power. You will be rolling on along loving rock's essence as it heals you, as it heals your soul.

Rock and roll might not help you get ahead in life, but it will make your life a whole lot more fun. So restart your life with rock and get ready for some rolling. Life's way too short, take it from me, learn from my mistakes. The rock's all good in Heaven but it still is not quite the same as it is on Earth. Trust me, your good looking, rock and roll Angel and hear these final words I say to you from my soul, You only truly live once. Mortal don't waste the years that you have left to live, being a dead minded person, a non rocker, believing only your way is the correct way to live. Because my dear lost friend, Heaven might not be your after life's destination. Believe this as truth, Hell is filled up full with the damned, praying to get out.

Do You Remember Rock And Roll / And What It Did
For You And Your Soul / It Kept You Young – Free And Hard
So Come Back To Rock / Start Rocking And Rolling Again

80

The Push That Got Away (Story Version)

A hot lady that is your lover, makes you feel so good, knowing that she's yours. A hot lady that loves you, makes greatness enter your life, knowing that you love her too. You get a big head, all nice and cocky when you're walking around with your fine love on your arm. Loving it strongly that you're making other men want to be you, having what you have, a hot lady that loves you and lets you have her. Turned on, you're the man, thinking to yourself that's right you wish, I receive, whenever I want.

(Flash forward to the next month.) Nancy is a Betty but I'm a real man, a man that has needs and greeds. (More cocky you've become.) She's not my wife, no matter how hot she is. I'm thinking it's time for some of the ever so popular, quantity over quality. There are so many ladies that want me, I'm hot, I'm on fire, I'm full of desire and best of all all the ladies I'll being choosing from, know what I'm use to. Happily they will give me their best. Nancy is hot, so sexy and wonderful to look at while I'm enjoying her, but she is missing a few spices that maybe another lady might possess. Then I'll have both of what I need for a more healthful, sexual life. Let me think, who should I give the pleasure and honor of pleasing me first. I'm so bad, but I'm so good and that is what is most important and having sex with someone that can keep a secret, will make me very happy. Who? Katie, Nancy's best friend? Yes, Katie. She told me once to give her a call, if Nancy ever decides to take off. Well I guess asleep in bed will have to do.

(A few hours later.) "Well Katie how great was I? No need to thank me, your silence is my reward for you. Now be a sweet thing and hand me my clothes and after that a sandwich and a beer would be great. Thank so very much, my new sweet-honey Katie." "You know what I'm thinking, Peter? I'm thinking that Nancy likes her man, your name with a little added to the front of it. Get your ass dressed and get the Hell out of here for I need a drink and after that I need to call Nancy and bitch her out on her very lacking choice for a boy friend."

(Ten minutes later) "Hello, Nancy my honey, what are you doing up?" "Peter you had it so lucky, I loved you even with all your short comings and no stamina at all, I would have stayed with you. You will never again in your life have it so great, now get the Hell out of here we're through." "I guess the bitch downed her drink."

The Push That Got Away / Was the Best Piece I Ever Had
I Would Love It If She Would Have Been / The Push That Stayed

81

Two Crazy Lovers (Story Version)

Jamie and Jimmy are not typical. They live their lives differently. They love each other, but they're desperate. They have no jobs and no Home. All they do is drive around, town to town looking for a John. Someone that is lonely enough to take Jamie home for the night. John gets what he wants, then when they can't go anymore and getting up seems like work. Jimmy comes walking in, knocks John over his head and he and Jamie tie up John so he can't move. Poor, stupid John wakes up to Jimmy looking really pissed, as a pretty little Jamie counts his money and sorts through his credit cards. Jamie gives John a kiss on the cheek goodbye, Jimmy simply pisses on John, as a fuck you.

(Here is an example of a John's night, that gets picked up by J and J. Let's start after Jamie and John has already had sex once.)

"Come on baby, you paid for me, is that all you want from me? Come on baby rock my world, give it to me better than you ever gave it to that fat wife of yours." "How did you know my wife is fat?" "John you are stupid. You almost finished before you really got started. I can tell you are not use to fine. I charged you thickly for my fine, so go ahead, the second ones on me or if you are not following me, I'm saying you can have me one more time for free."

"I don't think I should, I think I should get going home. Go ahead and keep the room for the night, feel free to use it as you please. Do I give you a tip?" "Tip? What am I a waitress? Get over here John and get yourself off again. You know you want me. Look at my body, it's barely been touched tonight. You don't want me to tell my next John that you could only go once. I think he would call you a bitch, while doing me for the third time, because John he is a real man." "My name ain't John?" "John you are stupid, shut up and prove to me you are a man that can make love more that once a night. a real man would do it even if it killed him. For, what a way to go."

At the end of the second time of sex. Jamie is humming a song to herself, wishing John was larger than a size 5. John however is not doing so good, he is pushing himself too hard, giving him a facial expression compared to holding back a painful fart.

John is done. "I can't believe this, I was great, I can't move." "Of course you can't move, you're fat, stupid and ugly. And you were not great, you were terrible."

82

Jamie gets up off the bed as John looks at her like, you bitch. Jamie keeps walking naked to the door of the hotel, she opens it up and yells, talks to Jimmy. "Jimmy hurry up and get the Hell in here and knock this John out. He was nasty and stinky, I need a shower." "Yes dear." "What the Hell is going on?' John cries out too tired from having sex to do anything but barely move. "Shut up, you defiled my Angel," Jimmy yells out as he take his miniature bat that is wrapped with electrical tape and places it heartily against John's soon to be hurting really bad head.

"Jamie you foul bitch, I can't you believe you picked up such a fat John." "Shut up you bastard! And whose fault is that? Yours that's who. Last night I picked up that fine and built John and what happened? You messed up by not hitting him hard enough and he almost got away. What a man that John was, he was still able to almost get away after making love to me three times. And Jimmy unlike this fat John he was much larger then a size 5, if you no what I mean?" "Shut up you slut." "Well I would not have to be a slut if you we're more of a man and had more money. But no you have to be as poor as you are stupid. So shut your ass up and tie up fat John here before he almost out runs you."

Being together for so many years Jamie and Jimmy, have been through it all. This crime spree that Jamie came up with is working good but it's making Jimmy feel sick, as he thinks about all the johns that Jamie is having sex with. In a few more weeks of night after night of Jamie having sex with John's has turned Jimmy crazy with jealousy. This makes Jimmy do things like tell Jamie no, no, no that one is not good enough, 'til Jamie says hell with it, when it starts to get late and picks out a new John for herself to roll. Jimmy can't stand to look at Jamie anymore, the look of complete satisfaction on her face is just too much for Jimmy to take anymore. Jimmy breaks downs and tells Jamie that this is over, he's going to get a regular job and take care of them.

Jamie laughs at Jimmy, telling him that he's out of his mind. Asking him what kind of job he could get that could possibly pay more than a night of love making and robbery. Jimmy stops the car in the middle of the road gets out, says good-bye Jamie and walks away. Jamie screams for Jimmy to get his ass back in the car and be a good boy for her. Jimmy just keeps on walking away making Jamie even madder. Then all of a sudden Jamie snaps as she jumps into the driver's seat. She puts the car into drive then stomps on the gas pedal and runs over Jimmy, at 39 miles and hour. Without a smile, Jamie drives away leaving Jimmy by the side of the road for the critters to eat.

Earth Prisoner (# Way Too Many) (Story Version)

I live on Earth alone, kicked off my planet, my sentence earth prisoner
way too many. I'm to live among the populace, just be a good non-
human, do no harm, make no money and survive barely. The Galaxy
Police, what a drag they are, they check on me constantly. There are
some of them now, better keep my head down, I've already had a
dealing with them a couple of days ago. I'm so hungry, damn Galaxy
Police, came into my home and they told me I was earning too much
money. They had their fun, all at my expense, destroying almost all of
my food, leaving me with small amounts of not enough to live on.

Wow these earth ladies look so tasty beautiful. Earth men are so damn
lucky, they get to go out and maybe meet some sweet thing, then maybe
get to make love to them. Earth men might get some crap sometimes in
the pursuit of sex. But not what I get. No, not at all. I get the crap
beaten out of me. I'm allowed to have sex if I want to. I have free will,
I'm told. But I also have to understand this, there are consequences.
Like after I have sex with an Earth woman, the Galaxy Police come to
my home the next morning, wake me up real fast, beat the crap
out of me with sticks, telling me how bad I've been. I even have to
freaking thank them or I will get my unfortunate ass taken out. What
can I say, I'm a lustful alien man, so I have many scars across my body,
from my many adventures with my clothes off.

My big problem is that I've been tagged. No way to get it out of me on
this planet, except by my own planet's technology. No way would any
of them do this, ever, the Galaxy Police have a perfect record. They
police us, they hate us because of us they have to be here, away from
their families. We are their trash that are allowed to barely live. A lot
of us are taken out daily. I think it's because so many bad people from
my former planet are being sent over to Earth. The Galaxy Police do
not have enough members of their force to handle the massive over
flow that our planet has been in over gear, sending over here.

Life Is Not Fair – My Planet Sucks
Earth Is Cool – The Beer and Weed Are Great
Only Damn Problem Is
I'm Earth Prisoner (# Way Too Many)
With No Way Of Ever Going Back Home Again
My Planet Sucks – I'm Going To Make Them Pay
It's Time – I Tell The Humans What's Going On

So many new rules are being forced upon us now, that are too easily broken. Because my ex-planet's government invents them as they think they are needed. Their desire to have a perfect planet, without anyone that says no to them is becoming less of a dream come true to a full bloom reality. My ex-planet's crazy power mad government have been so busy in clearing their planet of the unwanted, to take a real close look at what they have done. They have hatefully sent so many of us that there is no way now, that all of us will go unnoticed for much longer. The time is happening, I have to start something, bring my fellow aliens all together, unite with the humans to set us free.

Mankind of Earth don't like their own planet's people invading their own countries. They see this as an act of war. Mankind has had so many wars, with so many blood filled battles, to keep invaders out. What happens now is my ex-planet's fault. Myself and my group of alien brothers and sisters all together walk in union to inform the government of the U.S.A. about what is going on with their country and planet.

They listen very carefully, with wide open ears, as we tell them of our oppression. We agree to inform them of the whereabouts of all the members of the Galaxy Police that live among them inside their country. We are thanked for our loyalty to planet Earth, then we are taking away to spend some quality time together as we're housed all together as guest of the United States of America.

The U.S.A. informs many major countries as to what is going on and very bloodily the people of Earth eliminate almost all of the Galaxy Police, leaving only a few alive for questions and experiments.

What my stupid ex-planet did was start a galaxy war. In time, with help from us, the humans learned how to use our technology. They built themselves many, many space war ships. People of Earth flew off their planet with victory in their hearts. For the first time in human history, almost all of Earth's countries united under one massive powerful force. They attacked our ex-planet without mercy, after that they reaped all of its riches that our clean planet had to offer them

Life Is Not Fair – My Planet Sucks / Earth Is Cool – The Beer and
Weed Are Great / Only Damn Problem Is
I'm Earth Prisoner (# Way Too Many) / With No Way Of Ever
Going Back Home Again / My Planet Sucks / I'm Going To
Make Them Pay / It's Time – I Tell The Humans What's Going On

Blind Date #1 (A Lyrical Story Version)

Check this Out – I-Have-One
Crazy-Ass-Story to Tell-You
Starts-Off with a Co-worker
Giving-Me a Number of a Friend
Innocent-Enough – But-No-Freaking-Way
Made the Biggest-Mistake of My-Life

She was Hot – Dressed to Kill
I was All-Happy – Thinking-About
Getting-Myself – Some of That
Should have Listened to My-Mind
Instead of Mr. – Make-Her-Happy

When-She-Dragged-Me into Her-Home
Had-Me-Sit-Down as She-Kept
Changing-Outfit – After-Outfit
Just so I-Could – Help-Her-Find
The-Right-Outfit to Wear-That-Night

(Chorus)
No More – Never Again
What A Crazy Blind Date
This Crazy Lady Turned Out To Be
She Gave My Car Away
She Even Made Me – Get My Ass Kicked
While I Was Trying – To Get My Car Back

My-Blind-Date – Asked-Me if I was Thirsty
And-Right-Before – I-Could-Take a Drink
She-Grabbed the Glass – Out of My-Hand
And-Smashed it Against the Wall / Telling-Me – That it Was-Dirty
Then-She-Had-Me – Come into Her-Kitchen
Where-She-Tried to Get-Me – To-Drink-Some-Water
Out of Her-Freaking – Kitchen-Faucet

I-Told-Her – No-Thanks – She-Got-Mad
Yelled at Me to Look at Her-Tits
She-Then-Pulled-Down-Her-Pants and Bent-Over
Asking-Me – What-I-Thought of Them
Confused as Hell – I-Told-Her – They-Were-Great
As-I-Looked at Her-Ass – That-Had-Two-Pairs of
Panties on It – Both of Them – Different-Colors

She-Started-Laughing – Telling-Me
I-Don't-Know the Difference
Between-Tits and Ass and She-Hopes
That-I-know – What to Do – With-My-Pecker
Then-She-Says to Me – All-Seriously-Like
Give-Me-Pecker or Give-Me-Death
Over and Over – In-Different-Voices

(Chorus)
No More – Never Again
What A Crazy Blind Date
This Crazy Lady Turned Out To Be
She Gave My Car Away
She Even Made Me – Get My Ass Kicked
While I Was Trying – To Get My Car Back

After-Crazy-Lady's – Crazy-Chanting-Stopped
I-Was-Ready to Get the Hell – Out of There
But-Then-She-Licked-Her-Lips and Shook-Her-Hips
And-Stupidly – I-Walked-Out the Door with Her

We-Started-Our-Date-Outside – By-Me-Watching-Her
Take-Off-Running – Down the Sidewalk
As-Fast as She-Could – As-Soon as We-Stepped on It
I-Waited-Around to See – If-She-Would-Come-Back

Leaning-Against-My-Car – When-She-Came-Back
She was Giggling – Jumping-Up and Down
Yelling-Out-Loud – I-Did-It! – I-Did-It!
Being a Little – Pissed-Off – I-Said
Yeah – But-Can-You – Do-It-Again
She-Looked at Me – All-Confused
Then-She-Took-Off to Do-It-Again – Only to
Come-Back to Me – To-Do-It – All-Over-Again

When-She-Came-back the Third-Time
I-Didn't – Give a Damn
So-I-Said to Her – All-Ass-Like
That was Great – Crazy-Lady
Now-How-About – Some-Din-Din
Watching-You has Made-Me – Very-Hungry
She-Jumped-Back-Up and Down-Again
Yelling-Out – That-She-Wanted – Some-Din-Din

(Chorus)
No More – Never Again
What A Crazy Blind Date
This Crazy Lady Turned Out To Be
She Gave My Car Away
She Even Made Me – Get My Ass Kicked
While I Was Trying – To Get My Car Back

I-Made-Reservations at a Great-Place
But-Almost-Decided to Take-Her to a
Drive-Thru with a Talking-Clown
I-Laughed-Out-Loud – Thinking to Myself – What-Kind of
Conversation – She-Would-Have-With-It
Unfortunately – I-Took-Her to a Place
That had Real – Knives and Forks

Shouldn't-Have – Been-Surprised
When-She-Took-Them and
Stabbed the Table with Them
Saying-Out-Loud – Din-Din – Din-Din
Come-On-You-Bastards – Bring-Me – My-Din-Din
I-Want-My – Damn-Din-Din-Now

Smiling – Looking-Around – Embarrassed as Hell
I-Wanted to Calm-Her – So-I-Showed-Her – My-Napkin
Then with a Grand-Gesture – I-Showed it to Her
How it Looks – Unfolded – She-Smiled and
Grab it Out of My-Hand and Started to Play-With-It

The-Waiter-Comes-Up to Take-Our-Order
Jokingly-I-Ask-Him – What-They-Had in Finger-Foods
Only to be Told – Hard-Assed – That-They-Don't-Have-Any
So-I-Order-Us – Some-Kind of Chicken-Dish
Then-I-Said-Hell-With-It – Reach-Down – and Scratch-My-Balls

(Chorus)
No More – Never Again
What A Crazy Blind Date
This Crazy Lady Turned Out To Be
She Gave My Car Away
She Even Made Me – Get My Ass Kicked
While I Was Trying – To Get My Car Back

Dinner was Over – Yes-She-Played with Her-Food
She even Grabbed – Some of My-Dinner
So-Hers and Mine – Could-Have a Fight
Loser-Got-Thrown – On the Floor – Then-Stepped-On

Waiter-Came-Back to Ask-Us if We-Wanted-Dessert
Only to Slip and Fall – On the Losing-Chicken-Dinner
Knocking-Tables and People-Over
Before-Finally-Landing – Face-First on the Floor
I-Stood-Up – Walked-Over to Him and Grabbed the Check
I-Told-My-Laughing-Date to Stay-Right-There

When-I-Got-Back to Our-Table – She was Gone
So-I-Said-Out-Loud to Everybody
This was Fun and If-They-See-My
Crazy-Ass-Blind-Date – They-Could-Keep-Her

Going-Outside to Get-My-Car from the Valet
He-Tells-Me – That-My-Date – Already-Came and Picked-It-Up
Without-Thinking – I-Grabbed-Him and Start-Shaking-Him
Only to Stop and Tell-Him-Sorry it's Not-His-Fault
So-I-Looked-Around – Feeling-Like-Kicking – My-Own-Ass
Trying to Find – My-Car with One-Crazy-Ass-Bitch – Driving-It

(Chorus)
No More – Never Again
What A Crazy Blind Date
This Crazy Lady Turned Out To Be
She Gave My Car Away
She Even Made Me – Get My Ass Kicked
While I Was Trying – To Get My Car Back

I-Started-Walking before Asking – Which-Way-She-Went
I'm-About a Mile-Away – When-I-Spot-Her – Walking-Towards-Me
When-We-Reach-Each-Other – I-Have to Remind-Her – Who-I-Am
She-Tells-Me – There was a Bunch of Guys – Up-Ahead
That-Didn't-Have a Car so She-Gave-Them-Mine
I-Yelled-Where – She-Tells-Me and I-Go to Get-My – Car-Back

Finding-Them – It was Not a Surprise to Me
How-Happy-They-Were – Partying
With-My-Car – Like it Was – Their-Girlfriend
I-Tell-Them – This is My-Car and I'm-Taking it Back – And-I
Don't-Give a Damn – What-Some – Crazy-Bitch-Told-Them

89

Silence – A-Heartbeat-Later – I'm-Fighting-Five-Men
Too-Many-Fist – Too-Many-Feet – I-Bleed – I-Bleed
After-Awhile-They-Stop – Start-Laughing and Offer-Me a Beer
I-Drink it Down – Thankfully – Using-Some of It
To-Wash the Blood-Away – From-My-Face

My-Blind-Date-Walks-Up and Asks – If-I-Could-Drive-Her-Home
That-She is Bored-Now and She-Has – Had-Enough of Me
I'm-Getting-Ready to Tell-Her – What-She-Has to Do for a Ride
I-Stop-Myself – Thinking – She'll-Probably-Think
My Pecker is Some-Kind of Meat-Stick and Try to Eat-It

(Chorus)
No More – Never Again
What A Crazy Blind Date
This Crazy Lady Turned Out To Be
She Gave My Car Away
She Even Made Me – Get My Ass Kicked
While I Was Trying – To Get My Car Back

I-Take-My-Crazy-Ass-Date-Home – I-Even-Walk-Her to the Door
When-We-Reach-It – I-Come to Find-Out – That the Lady
That-Opens the Door – Was to Be – My-Real-Blind-Date
She had Been – Knocked-Out by My-Crazy-Date
Locked in Her-Bathroom and Had-All-Her
Makeup – Smeared-All-Over-Her-Face

Not a Surprise – That this Lady – I-Took-Out on a Date
Was-Wanted for Breaking into Other-Ladies'-Homes
She-Has-Done-This – Ten-Times – All-Over the State
I-Was-Told-This as I-Watched the Police – Take-Her-Away
Only to Watch-Her – Get-Away and Run-Down the Same
Sidewalk – She-Did-Earlier-That-Night – She-Ran so Damn-Fast
She-Sped-Herself – Out of Sight – I-Laughed – Walked-Away
Shaking-My-Head – Saying – Din-Din – Over and Over-Again

(Chorus)
No More – Never Again
What A Crazy Blind Date
This Crazy Lady Turned Out To Be
She Gave My Car Away
She Even Made Me – Get My Ass Kicked
While I Was Trying – To Get My Car Back

www.ingramcontent.com/pod-product-compliance
Lightning Source LLC
Chambersburg PA
CBHW070547030426
42337CB00016B/2390